A Tutorial on the Piecewise Regression Approach Applied to Bedload Transport Data

Sandra E. Ryan
Laurie S. Porth

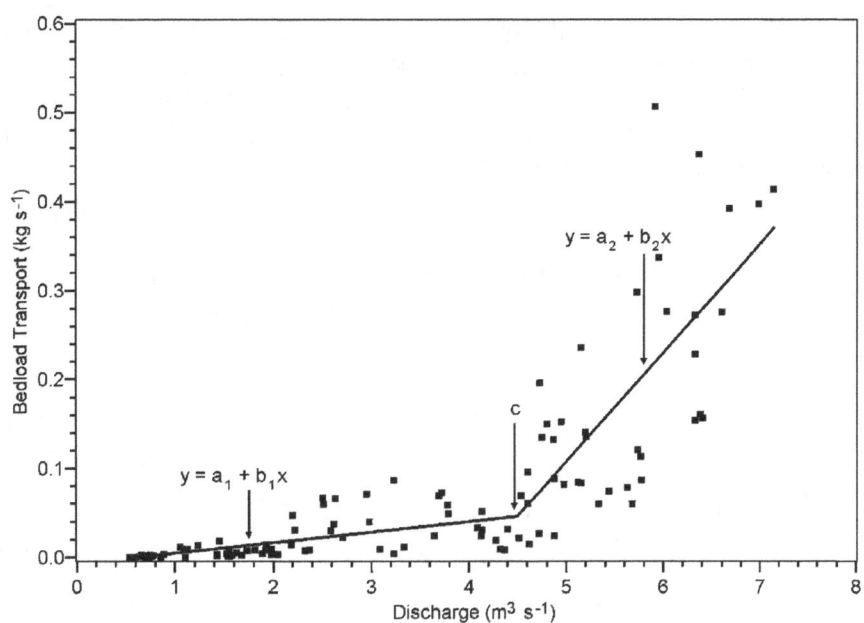

 United States
Department
of Agriculture

 Forest Service
Rocky Mountain Research Station

General Technical Report RMRS-GTR-189
May 2007

Ryan, Sandra E.; Porth, Laurie S. 2007. **A tutorial on the piecewise regression approach applied to bedload transport data.** Gen. Tech. Rep. RMRS-GTR-189. Fort Collins, CO: U.S. Department of Agriculture, Forest Service, Rocky Mountain Research Station. 41 p.

Abstract

This tutorial demonstrates the application of piecewise regression to bedload data to define a shift in phase of transport so that the reader may perform similar analyses on available data. The use of piecewise regression analysis implicitly recognizes different functions fit to bedload data over varying ranges of flow. The transition from primarily low rates of sand transport (Phase I) to higher rates of sand and coarse gravel transport (Phase II) is termed "breakpoint" and is defined as the flow where the fitted functions intersect. The form of the model used here fits linear segments to different ranges of data, though other types of functions may be used. Identifying the transition in phases is one approach used for defining flow regimes that are essential for self-maintenance of alluvial gravel bed channels. First, the statistical theory behind piecewise regression analysis and its procedural approaches are presented. The reader is then guided through an example procedure and the code for generating an analysis in SAS is outlined. The results from piecewise regression analysis from a number of additional bedload datasets are presented to help the reader understand the range of estimated values and confidence limits on the breakpoint that the analysis provides. The identification and resolution of problems encountered in bedload datasets are also discussed. Finally, recommendations on a minimal number of samples required for the analysis are proposed.

Keywords: Piecewise linear regression, breakpoint, bedload transport

Authors

Sandra E. Ryan, Research Hydrologist/Geomorphologist
U.S. Forest Service
Rocky Mountain Research Station
240 West Prospect Road
Fort Collins, CO 80526
E-mail: sryanburkett@fs.fed.us
Phone: 970-498-1015
Fax: 970-498-1212

Laurie S. Porth, Statistician
U.S. Forest Service
Rocky Mountain Research Station
240 West Prospect Road
Fort Collins, CO 80526
E-mail: lporth@fs.fed.us
Phone: 970-498-1206
Fax: 970-498-1212

Statistical code and output shown in boxed text in the document (piecewise regression procedure and bootstrapping), as well as an electronic version of the Little Granite Creek dataset are available on the Stream System Technology Center website under
"software" at http://stream.fs.fed.us/publications/software.html.

Contents

Introduction

Bedload transport in coarse-bedded streams is an irregular process influenced by a number of factors, including spatial and temporal variability in coarse sediment available for transport. Variations in measured bedload have been attributed to fluctuations occurring over several scales, including individual particle movement (Bunte 2004), the passing of bedforms (Gomez and others 1989, 1990), the presence of bedload sheets (Whiting and others 1988), and larger pulses or waves of stored sediment (Reid and Frostick 1986). As a result, rates of bedload transport can exhibit exceptionally high variability, often up to an order of magnitude or greater for a given discharge. However, when rates of transport are assessed for a wide range of flows, there are relatively predictable patterns in many equilibrium gravel-bed channels.

Coarse sediment transport has been described as occurring in phases, where there are distinctly different sedimentological characteristics associated with flows under different phases of transport. At least two phases of bedload transport have been described (Emmett 1976). Under Phase I transport, rates are relatively low and consist primarily of sand and a few small gravel particles that are considerably finer than most of the material comprising the channel bed. Phase I likely represents re-mobilization of fine sediment deposited from previous transport events in pools and tranquil areas of the bed (Paola and Seal 1995, Lisle 1995). Phase II transport represents initiation and transport of grains from the coarse surface layer common in steep mountain channels, and consists of sand, gravel, and some cobbles moved over a stable or semi-mobile bed. The beginning of Phase II is thought to occur at or near the "bankfull" discharge (Parker 1979; Parker and others 1982; Jackson and Beschta 1982; Andrews 1984; Andrews and Nankervis 1995), but the threshold is often poorly or subjectively defined.

Ryan and others (2002, 2005) evaluated the application of a piecewise regression model for objectively defining phases of bedload transport and the discharge at which there is a substantial change in the nature of sediment transport in gravel bed streams. The analysis recognizes the existence of different transport relationships for different ranges of flow. The form of the model used in these evaluations fit linear segments to the ranges of flow, though other types of functions may be used. A *breakpoint* was defined by the flow where the fitted functions intersected. This was interpreted as the transition between phases of transport. Typically, there were markedly different statistical and sedimentological features associated with flows that were less than or greater than the breakpoint discharge. The fitted line for less-than-breakpoint flows had a lower slope with less variance due to the fact that bedload at these discharges consisted primarily of small quantities of sand-sized materials. In contrast, the fitted line for flows greater than the breakpoint had a significantly steeper slope and more variability in transport rates due to the physical breakup of the armor layer, the availability of subsurface material, and subsequent changes in both the size and volume of sediment in transport.

Defining the breakpoint or shift from Phase I to Phase II using measured rates of bedload transport comprises one approach for defining flow regimes essential for self-maintenance of alluvial gravel bed channels (see Schmidt and Potyondy 2004 for full description of channel maintenance approach). The goal of this tutorial is to demonstrate the application of piecewise regression to bedload data so that the reader may perform similar analyses on available data. First we present statistical theory behind piecewise regression and its procedural approaches. We guide the reader through an example procedure and provide the code for generating an analysis using SAS (2004), which is a statistical analysis software package. We then present the results from a number of examples using additional bedload datasets to give the reader an understanding of the range of estimated values and confidence limits on the breakpoint that this analysis provides. Finally, we discuss recommendations on minimal number of samples required, and the identification and resolution of problems encountered in bedload datasets.

Data

Data on bedload transport and discharge used in this application were obtained through a number of field studies conducted on small to medium sized gravel-bedded rivers in Colorado and Wyoming. The characteristics of channels from which the data originate and the methods for collecting the data are fully described in Ryan and others (2002, 2005). Flow and rate of bedload transport are the primary variables used in the assessment of the breakpoint. Bedload was collected using hand-held bedload samplers, either while wading or, more typically, from sampling platforms constructed at the channel cross-sections. Mean flow during the period of sample collection was obtained from a nearby gaging station or from flow rating curves established for the sites.

Statistical Theory

When analyzing a relationship between a response, y, and an explanatory variable, x, it may be apparent that for different ranges of x, different linear relationships occur. In these cases, a single linear model may not provide an adequate description and a nonlinear model may not be appropriate either. Piecewise linear regression is a form of regression that allows multiple linear models to be

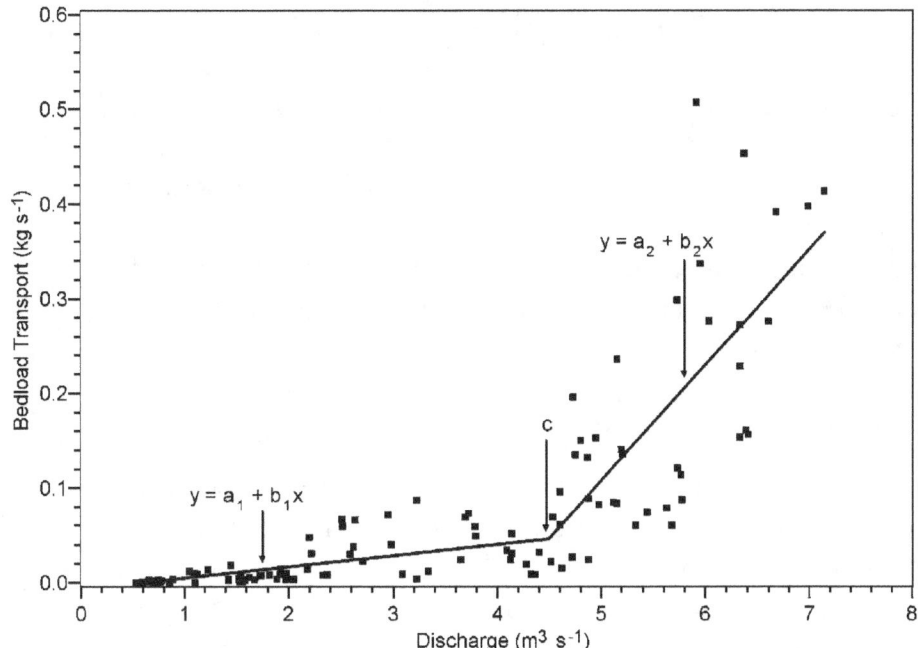

Figure 1—Example of a piecewise regression fit between discharge and bedload transport data collected at St. Louis Creek Site 2, Fraser Experimental Forest (Ryan and others 2002).

fit to the data for different ranges of x. Breakpoints are the values of x where the slope of the linear function changes (fig. 1). The value of the breakpoint may or may not be known before the analysis, but typically it is unknown and must be estimated. The regression function at the breakpoint may be discontinuous, but a model can be written in such a way that the function is continuous at all points including the breakpoints. Given what is understood about the nature of bedload transport, we assume the function should be continuous. When there is only one breakpoint, at $x=c$, the model can be written as follows:

$$y = a_1 + b_1 x \qquad \text{for } x \leq c$$
$$y = a_2 + b_2 x \qquad \text{for } x > c.$$

In order for the regression function to be continuous at the breakpoint, the two equations for y need to be equal at the breakpoint (when $x = c$):

$$a_1 + b_1 c = a_2 + b_2 c.$$

Solve for one of the parameters in terms of the others by rearranging the equation above:

$$a_2 = a_1 + c(b_1 - b_2).$$

Then by replacing a_2 with the equation above, the result is a piecewise regression model that is continuous at $x = c$:

$$y = a_1 + b_1 x \qquad \text{for } x \leq c$$
$$y = \{a_1 + c(b_1 - b_2)\} + b_2 x \qquad \text{for } x > c.$$

Nonlinear least squares regression techniques, such as PROC NLIN in SAS, can be used to fit this model to the data.

Tutorial Examples

In order to run the examples from these tutorials the user must have some knowledge of SAS, such as the ability to move around in the SAS environment and import data. SAS version 9.1.3 was used to implement these programs. Most of this code will work with SAS versions beginning with 8.2, but it is important to note that the nonlinear regression procedure used to fit the models was modified between versions 8.2 and 9, and this can produce slight differences in the final results.

Little Granite Creek Example

Data from Little Granite Creek near Jackson, Wyoming were collected by William Emmett and staff from the U.S. Geological Survey from 1982 through 1992. Sandra Ryan of the U.S. Forest Service, Rocky Mountain Research Station collected additional data during high runoff in 1997. This dataset has over 120 observations from a wide range of flows (Appendix A) (Ryan and Emmett 2002).

Estimating starting parameters

The first step in applying piecewise regression to bedload and flow data is to graph the data and estimate where the breaks appear to occur. Applying a nonparametric smooth to the data, such as a LOESS fit (box 1), can help the user determine where these breaks manifest themselves. Using figure 2, we visually estimate the breakpoint to be somewhere between 4.0 and 8.0 m^3 s^{-1}.

Box 1. Apply a nonparametric smooth to the data and generate figure 2.

```
* -- USE LOESS PROCEDURE TO GET SMOOTHED NONPARAMETRIC FIT OF DATA -- *;
PROC LOESS DATA=ltlgran;
   MODEL Y=X;
   ODS OUTPUT OUTPUTSTATISTICS=LOESSFIT;
RUN;
* -- PLOT DATA AND THE LOESS FIT -- *;
SYMBOL1 f=marker v=U i=none c=black;
SYMBOL2 v=none i=join line=1 w=3 c=black;
AXIS2 label = (a=90 r=0);
PROC GPLOT DATA=LOESSFIT;
   PLOT DEPVAR*X=1 PRED*X=2 / OVERLAY FRAME VAXIS=AXIS2;
RUN;
```

A standard linear regression model is then fit to the entire data range (fig. 3, box 2). It is apparent the linear model is a poor fit over the entire range of discharges because the values obtained at lower flows do not fall along the line. The results from this model (box 2) will be used as a baseline to compare with the piecewise model. To be acceptable, the piecewise model should account for more variability than the linear model.

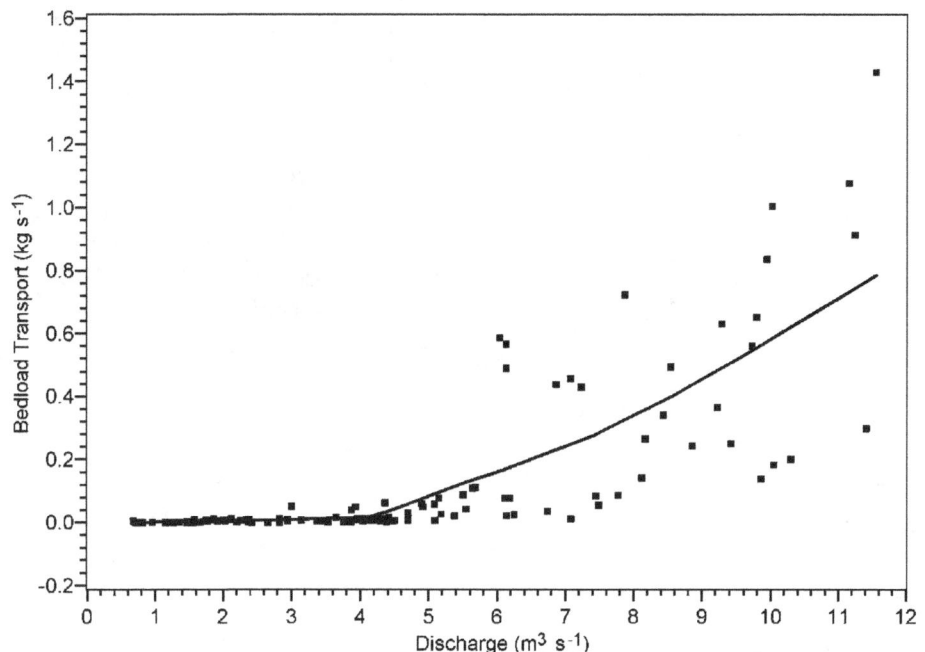

Figure 2—Loess fit between discharge and bedload transport data collected at Little Granite Creek.

Box 2. Apply a linear regression model to the data and generate figure 3.

```
* -- APPLY LINEAR REGRESSION MODEL TO THE DATA -- *;
PROC REG DATA=ltlgran;
   MODEL Y=X;
   OUTPUT OUT=LINEARFIT P=PRED;
RUN;
* -- PLOT DATA AND THE LINEAR REGRESSION FIT -- *;
SYMBOL1 f=marker v=U i=none c=black;
SYMBOL2 v=none i=join line=1 w=3 c=black;
AXIS2 label = (a=90 r=0);
PROC GPLOT DATA=LINEARFIT;
   PLOT Y*X=1 PRED*X=2 / OVERLAY FRAME VAXIS=AXIS2;
RUN;
```

Analysis of Variance – Linear Model

Source	DF	Sum of Squares	Mean Square	F Value	Pr > F
Model	1	4.25406	4.25406	138.95	<.0001
Error	121	3.70441	0.03061		
Corrected Total	122	7.95847			

Root MSE	0.17497	R-Square	0.5345	
Dependent Mean	0.12540	Adj R-Sq	0.5307	
Coeff Var	139.53045			

Starting parameters (a_1, b_1, b_2, c) are needed in the PROC NLIN procedure to give the program a place to begin fitting the model. Poor starting parameters

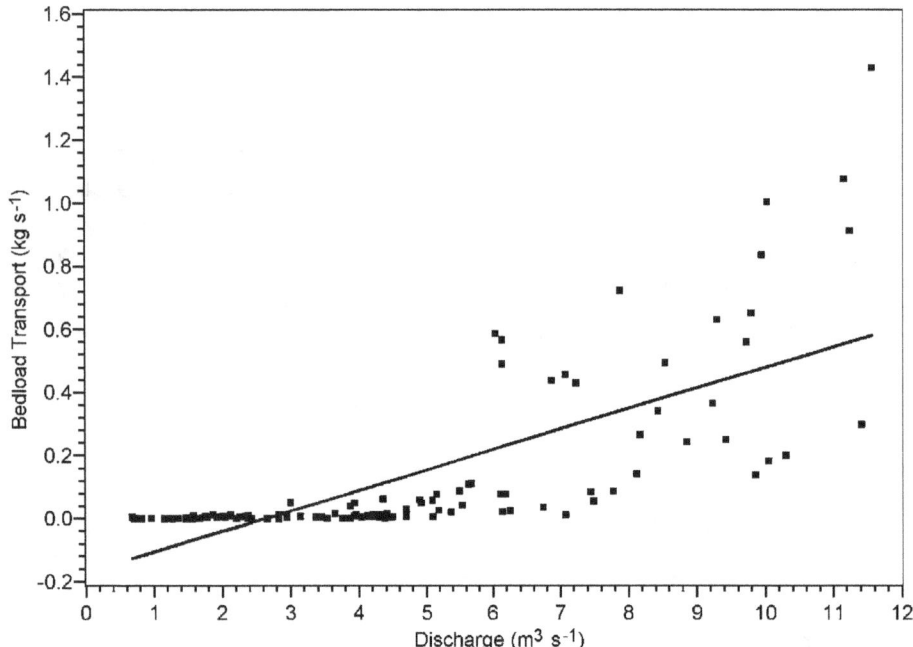

Figure 3—Linear fit between discharge and bedload transport data collected at Little Granite Creek.

may result in non-convergence, so this is an important step. Starting parameters are provided by estimating a simple linear model separately above and below the estimated breakpoint location (fig. 4, box 3). Because the estimated break-point appears to be somewhere between 4.0 and 8.0 m^3 s^{-1} (from fig. 2), it is best to estimate starting parameters at multiple points between 4.0 and 8.0, and then choose the model with the best fit (in other words, has the smallest mean

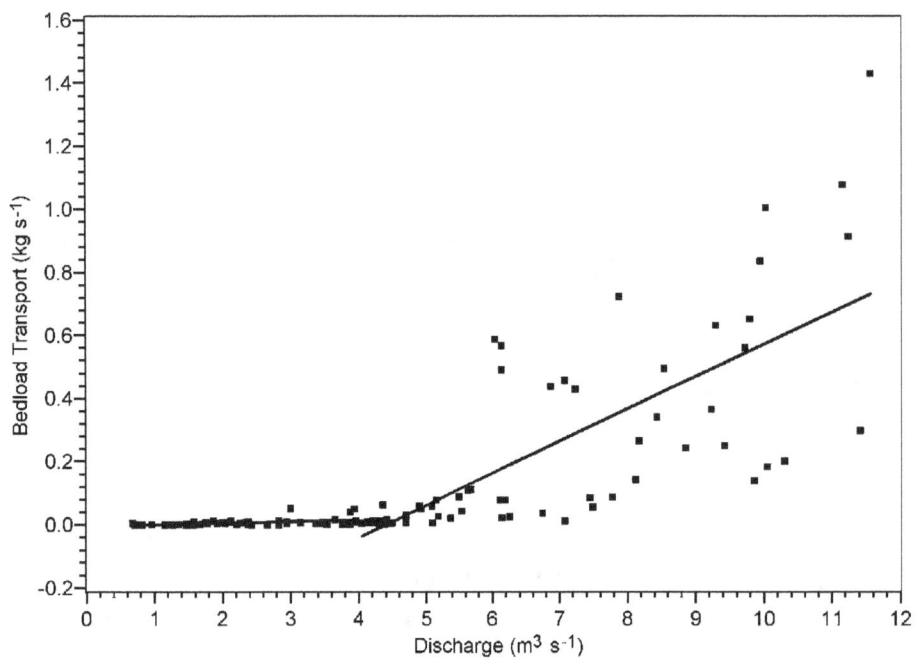

Figure 4—Linear fits between discharge and bedload transport data below and above an estimated breakpoint of 4.0. Data from Little Granite Creek.

USDA Forest Service RMRS-GTR-189. 2007

squared error). We obtained initial starting parameters for models where the breakpoint was 4.0, 6.0 (half-way), and 8.0.

Box 3. Apply two linear regression models to the data and generate figure 4.

```
* -- APPLY LINEAR REG MODEL TO DATA BELOW ESTIMATED BREAKPOINT -- *;
PROC REG DATA=ltlgran;
  MODEL Y=X;
  OUTPUT OUT=FITBELOW P=PREDBELOW;
  WHERE X <= 4.0;
RUN;
* -- APPLY LINEAR REG MODEL TO DATA ABOVE ESTIMATED BREAKPOINT -- *;
PROC REG DATA=ltlgran;
  MODEL Y=X;
  OUTPUT OUT=FITABOVE P=PREDABOVE;
  WHERE X > 4.0;
RUN;
* -- COMBINE DATASETS -- *;
DATA FITBOTH;
  SET FITBELOW FITABOVE;
RUN;
* -- PLOT DATA AND THE TWO LINEAR REGRESSION FITS -- *;
SYMBOL1 f=marker v=U i=none c=black;
SYMBOL2 v=none i=join line=1 w=3 c=black;
AXIS2 label = (a=90 r=0);
PROC GPLOT DATA=FITBOTH;
  PLOT Y*X=1 PREDBELOW*X=2 PREDABOVE*X=2 / OVERLAY FRAME VAXIS=AXIS2;
RUN;
```

Linear Fit **Below** Estimated Breakpoint=4.0

Variable	Label	DF	Parameter Estimate	Standard Error	t Value	Pr > |t|
Intercept	Intercept	1	-0.00422	0.00307	-1.37	0.1749
X	Discharge (cubic meters/sec)	1	0.00473	0.00128	3.70	0.0005

Linear Fit **At and Above** Estimated Breakpoint=4.0

Variable	Label	DF	Parameter Estimate	Standard Error	t Value	Pr > |t|
Intercept	Intercept	1	-0.45074	0.08280	-5.44	<.0001
X	Discharge (cubic meters/sec)	1	0.10221	0.01174	8.71	<.0001

The estimated starting parameters for the piecewise model,

$$y = a_1 + b_1 x \qquad for\ x \le c$$
$$y = \{a_1 + c(b_1 - b_2)\} + b_2 x \qquad for\ x > c.$$

and the methods used to obtain them are shown in table 1.

Table 1—Estimated piecewise regression starting parameters for a breakpoint at 4.0.

Parameter	Estimated starting parameter	How obtained
a_1	-0.00422	Intercept of linear fit to data below estimated breakpoint.
b_1	0.00473	Slope of linear fit to data below estimated breakpoint.
b_2	0.10221	Slope of linear fit to data above estimated breakpoint.
c	4.0	Estimated breakpoint from LOESS plot.

Fitting the model

The starting parameters are then used to fit the piecewise regression model with PROC NLIN procedure in SAS (fig. 5, box 4).

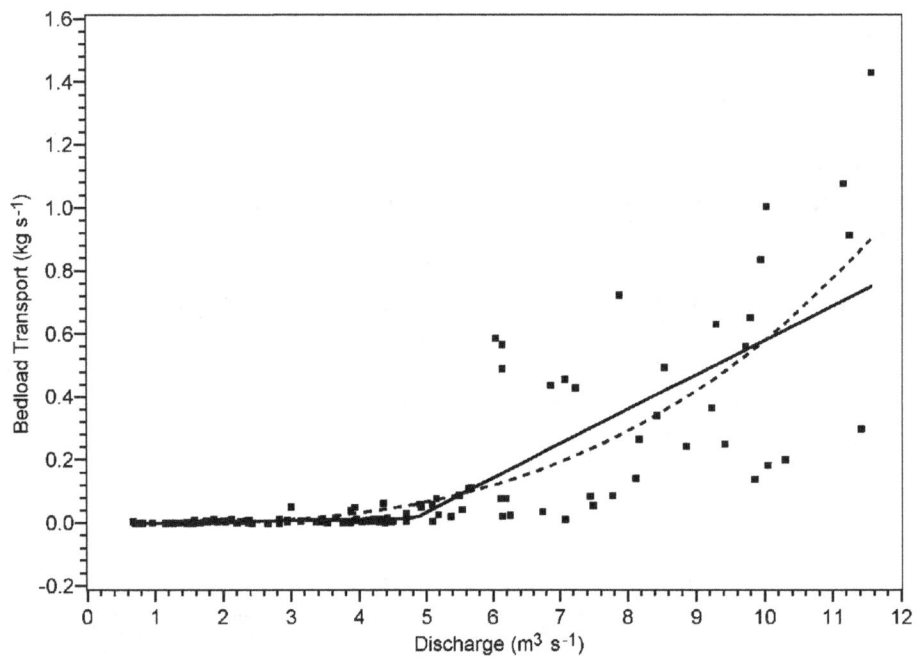

Figure 5—Piecewise regression between discharge and bedload transport data collected at Little Granite Creek. A power function is shown for comparison.

USDA Forest Service RMRS-GTR-189. 2007

Box 4. Apply a piecewise and power model to the data and generate figure 5.

```
* -- FIT THE PIECEWISE MODEL USING NONLINEAR PROCEDURE -- *;
PROC NLIN DATA=ltlgran MAXITER=1000 METHOD=MARQUARDT;
   PARMS a1=-0.00422 b1=0.00473 c=4 b2=0.10221;
   Xpart = a1 + b1*X;
   IF (X > c) THEN DO;
      Xpart = a1 + c*(b1-b2) + b2*X;
      end;
   MODEL Y = Xpart;
   OUTPUT OUT=PIECEFIT R=RESID P=PRED;
RUN;
* -- FIT THE POWER MODEL (FOR COMPARISON) USING NONLINEAR PROCEDURE -- *;
PROC NLIN DATA=ltlgran MAXITER=1000 METHOD=MARQUARDT;
   PARMS a1=0.01 b1=0.01 b2=1.0;
   MODEL Y = a1 + b1*X**b2;
   OUTPUT OUT=POWERFIT R=PWR_RESID P=PWR_PRED;
RUN;
* -- COMBINE OUTPUT FROM BOTH MODELS -- *;
DATA ALL;
   SET PIECEFIT POWERFIT;
RUN;
* -- PLOT DATA, PIECEWISE REGRESSION FIT, AND POWER MODEL FIT -- *;
SYMBOL1 f=marker v=U i=none c=black;
SYMBOL2 v=none i=join line=1 w=3 c=black;
SYMBOL3 v=none i=join line=2 w=3 c=black;
AXIS2 label = (a=90 r=0);
PROC GPLOT DATA=ALL;
   PLOT Y*X=1 PRED*X=2 PWR_PRED*X=3 / OVERLAY FRAME VAXIS=AXIS2;
RUN;
```

Little Granite Creek
Piecewise Regression Fit
The NLIN Procedure
Dependent Variable Y
Method: Marquardt
Iterative Phase

Iter	a1	b1	c	b2	Sum of Squares
0	-0.0150	0.00949	6.0000	0.1081	3.2790
1	-0.0150	0.00949	4.9368	0.1081	2.8875
2	-0.00484	0.00485	4.9114	0.1104	2.8825
3	-0.00377	0.00432	4.8794	0.1100	2.8822
4	-0.00223	0.00355	4.8340	0.1094	2.8820
5	-0.00223	0.00355	4.8341	0.1094	2.8820

NOTE: Convergence criterion met.

Source	DF	Sum of Squares	Mean Square	Approx F Value	Pr > F
Model	3	5.0765	1.6922	69.87	<.0001
Error	119	2.8820	0.0242		
Corrected Total	122	7.9585			

Parameter	Estimate	Approx Std Error	Approximate 95% Confidence Limits	
a1	-0.00223	0.0423	-0.0860	0.0815
b1	0.00355	0.0141	-0.0244	0.0315
c	4.8341	0.4977	3.8486	5.8197
b2	0.1094	0.0115	0.0867	0.1320

Under the "Iterative Phase" of the output, there is a note indicating "Convergence criterion met." This means the model converged and a breakpoint of 4.83 and a mean squared error (MSE) of 0.0242 were estimated. If we repeat the above series of steps for breakpoints at 6.0 and 8.0, we get models that converge with breakpoints at 4.83 (with MSE=0.0242), which is the same model produced with an initial breakpoint of 4.0, and 8.27 (with MSE=0.0246), respectively. The models that converged with a breakpoint of 4.83 have the smallest MSE and therefore the best fit.

The results from the piecewise regression model are then compared with those from the linear model (fig. 3). An extra sums of squares test (Neter and others 1990) can be used to determine if the piecewise regression model is an improvement over the linear model. Other models can also be compared, such as a power model (also shown in fig. 5) commonly used in fitting bedload data (Whiting and others 1999). However, there is no formal test available that allows the direct comparison of a piecewise regression model to a power model, but one can compare the results using the model standard error, also known as the square root of the mean squared error. This is the average distance of each observation from the fitted model and smaller values indicate an improved fit. The results from curve fits to the Little Granite Creek data are compared in table 2.

Table 2—Model standard errors for the linear, power, and piecewise regression models for Little Granite Creek.

Least squares model	Model standard error
Linear: $y = a_1 + b_1 x$	0.0306
Power: $y = a_1 + b_1 x^{b_2}$	0.0230
Piecewise	0.0242

Based on comparisons of the model standard error and the visual fit, the linear model is clearly not the best fit. However, the model standard error for the piecewise linear model isn't substantially different from the power model. Justification for using the piecewise regression model in this case would be based on scientific reasons (Bates and Watts 1988). That is, if the piecewise regression model has approximately the same goodness of fit as a different model, then scientific reasoning could be used to select the model. In this case, we choose the piecewise model to objectively determine the onset of different phases of bedload transport that have been shown to exist in many gravel bed rivers.

Testing model assumptions

The next step is to ensure that the assumptions of the model have been met. The first assumption in regression analysis is the <u>independence of the residuals</u>

(which are the actual-y minus predicted-y values), meaning the value of one residual is unrelated to the value of the next. As an example of dependence, bedload samples are often taken in the field over relatively short time intervals (hours to days), causing potential correlation between discharge values due to time. If the values of x are correlated, then the residuals will be correlated. Neter and others (1990) state that if the data are correlated, the regression coefficients are still unbiased but may be inefficient, and the mean squared error and standard deviations of the parameters may be seriously underestimated. A plot of the residuals over time should show no trends, otherwise the assumed independence of the x values is violated. The Little Granite Creek dataset contains data ranging from April through July for 1985 through 1997. It is difficult to show trends on a single plot for such a lengthy period of record, so for simplicity we plot the data sequentially assuming equal distance between the measurements (box 5).

Box 5. Check residuals for independence by generating figure 6.

```
* -- SORT THE DATA BY TIME -- *;
PROC SORT DATA=PIECEFIT;
   BY date;
RUN;
* -- ADD A DUMMY TIME VARIABLE TO MAKE PLOTTING EASIER -- *;
DATA PIECEFIT;
   RETAIN TIME 0;
   SET PIECEFIT;
   TIME = TIME + 1;
RUN;
* -- PLOT THE RESIDUALS OVER TIME IN ORDER TO CHECK FOR INDEPENDENCE -- *;
SYMBOL1 f=marker v=U i=join c=black;
AXIS2 label = (a=90 r=0);
PROC GPLOT DATA=PIECEFIT;
   PLOT X*TIME=1 / FRAME VAXIS=AXIS2;
RUN;
```

From the graph of the residuals over time (fig. 6), it is apparent there may be some correlation because the residuals are not randomly scattered above and below zero. For instance, around time 100 there are nine consecutive data points below zero and then eleven consecutive data points above zero. One way to check for correlation is to model the residuals using an autoregressive [AR(1)] variance structure, which takes into account that a particular observation is correlated with the previous observation (box 6). In other words, we can better predict the value of the current observation if we use the value of the previous observation. If there is a substantial difference between this adjusted MSE (which is the valid MSE for the model) and the MSE from the original piecewise regression model, then the implication is that the residuals are correlated. Setting SUBJECT=year tells SAS there is no correlation between years.

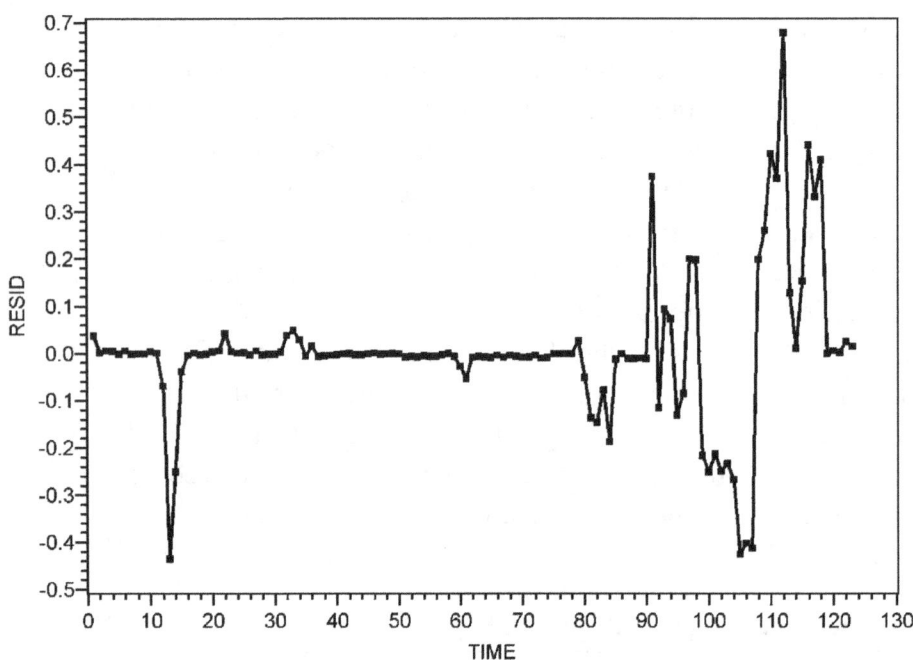

Figure 6—Piecewise regression residuals for Little Granite Creek plotted sequentially to check for independence.

The data for this particular site represent approximately April through July of each year and we would not expect the July measurement to be correlated with April measurement of the following year. Assuming only the correlation within each year, the estimate for the correlation parameter is 0.6194 (box 6), and the Wald Z-test shows a significant p-value (p<0.0001). This means the residuals are significantly correlated, and the MSE is actually 0.0226. The MSE from the piecewise regression model was 0.0242, which is only a 7 percent difference so we assume the effects of correlation are not substantial.

Box 6. Apply an autoregressive model to the residuals.

```
*-- SORT THE DATA BY TIME -- *;
PROC SORT DATA=PIECEFIT;
   BY date;
RUN;
* -- MODEL THE RESIDUALS AS AN AR(1) -- *;
PROC MIXED DATA=PIECEFIT;
   MODEL RESID=;
   REPEATED / SUBJECT=year TYPE=AR(1);
RUN;
```

Little Granite Creek
GET MSE ADJUSTED FOR CORRELATION
Convergence criteria met.
Covariance Parameter Estimates

Cov Parm	Subject	Estimate	Standard Error	Z Value	Pr Z	Alpha	Lower	Upper
AR(1)	YEAR	0.6194	0.06630	9.34	<.0001	0.05	0.4895	0.7493
Residual		0.02256	0.004031	5.60	<.0001	0.05	0.01635	0.03313

A second assumption is that the <u>residuals exhibit normality</u>. This means the error in the model prediction, which is the distribution of the residuals, should appear to be a bell-shaped curve (a normal distribution) with many "average" sized residuals and fewer large and small residuals. Too many extreme values, small or large, suggest a skewed distribution. A visual way to determine if the residuals follow the normal distribution is to generate a QQ-plot, which is a graph of the quantiles of the normal distribution against the quantiles of the data (box 7). If the data closely match the quantiles of the normal distribution, then the data are normal. With a piecewise regression model, which consists of two linear models, we examine the residuals below and then above the breakpoint (fig. 7).

Box 7. Check residuals for normality and generate figure 7.

```
* -- CHECK RESIDUALS FOR NORMALITY BELOW THE BREAKPOINT -- *;
SYMBOL1 f=marker v=U i=none c=black;
PROC UNIVARIATE DATA=PIECEFIT NORMAL;
   WHERE (X <= 4.83);
   VAR RESID;
   QQPLOT RESID / NORMAL(MU=EST SIGMA=EST);
RUN;
* -- CHECK RESIDUALS FOR NORMALITY ABOVE THE BREAKPOINT -- *;
PROC UNIVARIATE DATA=PIECEFIT NORMAL;
   WHERE (X > 4.83);
   VAR RESID;
   QQPLOT RESID / NORMAL(MU=EST SIGMA=EST);
RUN;
```

Tests for Normality
Checking for Normality Below the Breakpoint

Test	-------Statistic--------		-----------p Value-----------	
Shapiro-Wilk	W	0.659789	Pr < W	<0.0001
Kolmogorov-Smirnov	D	0.24104	Pr > D	<0.0100
Cramer-von Mises	W-Sq	1.268588	Pr > W-Sq	<0.0050
Anderson-Darling	A-Sq	7.403709	Pr > A-Sq	<0.0050

Tests for Normality
Checking for Normality Above the Breakpoint

Test	--------Statistic-------		-----------p Value-----------	
Shapiro-Wilk	W	0.970409	Pr < W	0.2869
Kolmogorov-Smirnov	D	0.113803	Pr > D	0.1387
Cramer-von Mises	W-Sq	0.068001	Pr > W-Sq	>0.2500
Anderson-Darling	A-Sq	0.424133	Pr > A-Sq	>0.2500

The visual interpretation of the two plots suggests that the residuals of the data below the breakpoint (fig. 7a) are not normal, while the data above the breakpoint (fig. 7b) exhibit a near one-to-one relationship between the data and the normal distribution. Another way to check for normality is to use the Shapiro-Wilk test (among others in box 7). The results from this test show that the residuals below the breakpoint are, indeed, not normal ($p<0.0001$), but we cannot reject normality for the residuals above the breakpoint ($p=0.2869$).

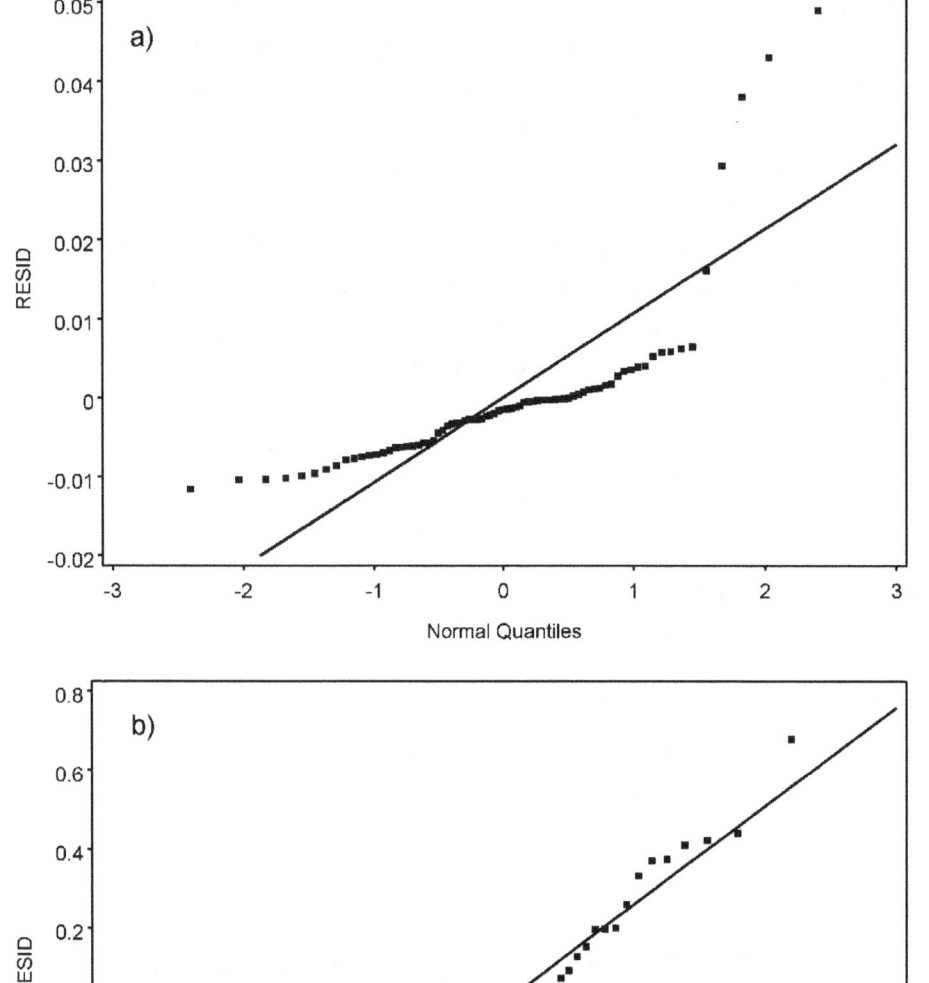

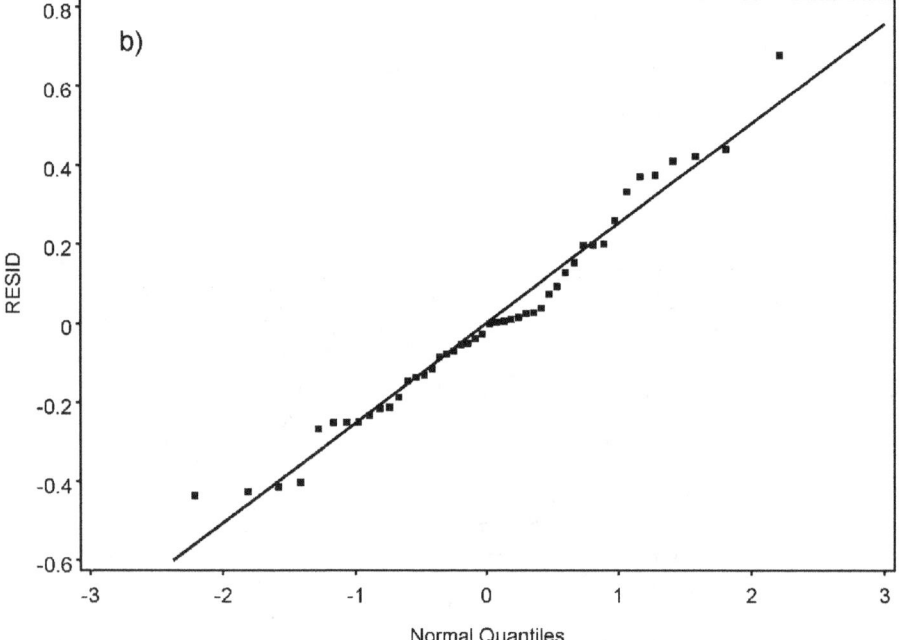

Figure 7—QQ-plots for Little Granite Creek piecewise regression residuals for curves fit to data (a) below and (b) above the break-point value.

A third assumption is that <u>residuals have homogeneous variance</u>, with the variability of the residuals between and within the fitted segments being approximately constant. By plotting the residuals on the y-axis and the predicted fit on the x-axis, one can determine if the variability of the data is constant across the entire range of x (fig. 8, box 8). The linearity assumption, where an equal number of data points randomly occur on either side of the model, can also be examined using the plot of the residuals versus the predicted values. Figure 8(a and b) shows nearly half the data points are below and half above the line. Hence, the linearity of the two segments is not in question. However, it is apparent the residuals are not homogeneous because the variance increases with the predicted value. The reader is referred to Neter and others (1990) for additional explanation of the assumptions of a regression model.

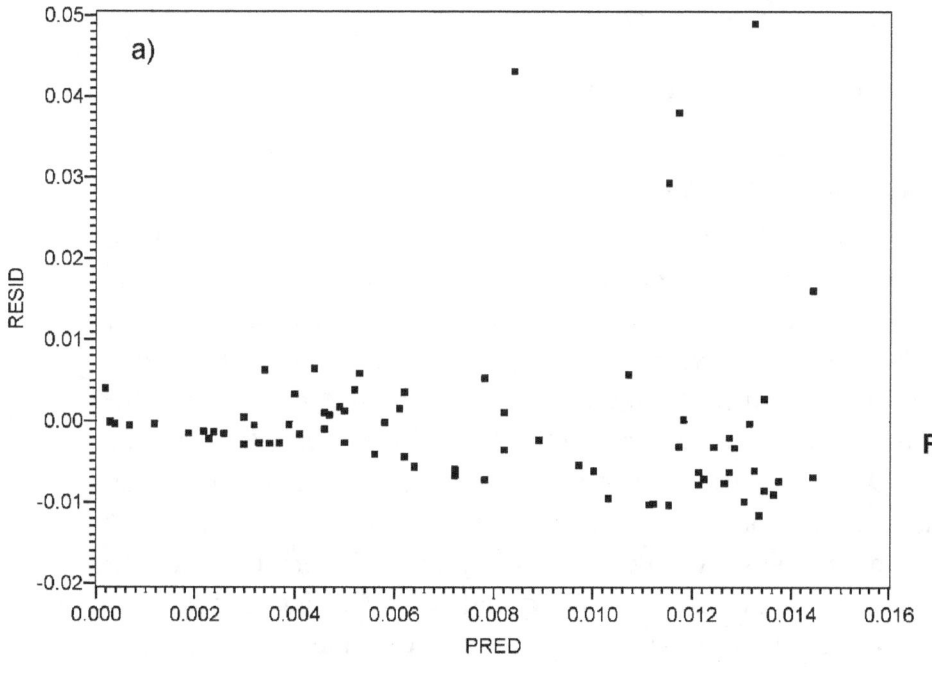

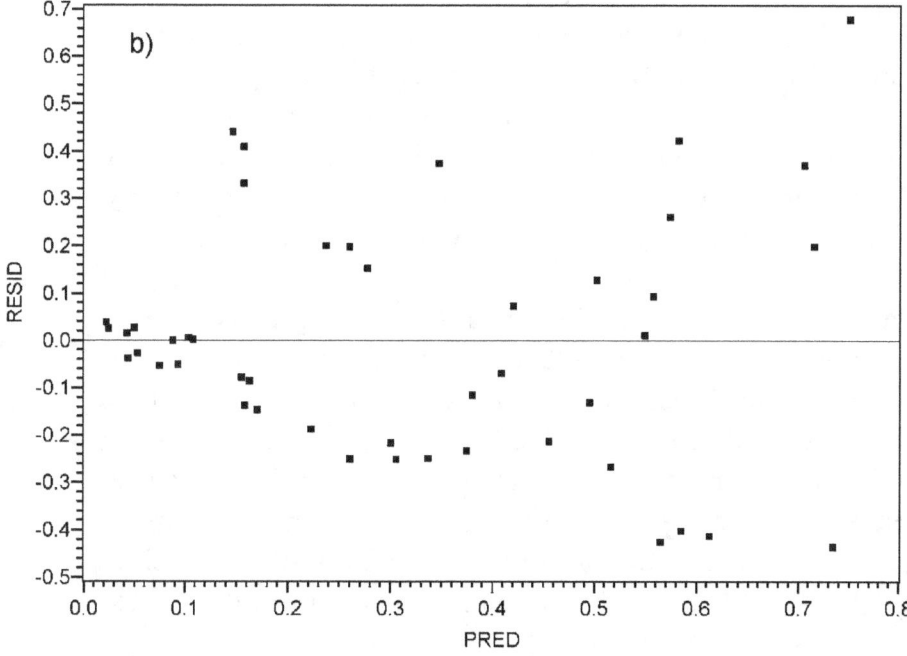

Figure 8—Little Granite Creek piecewise regression residuals and predicted values (a) below and (b) above the breakpoint.

```
Box 8. Check residuals for lack of fit and heterogeneous variance and generate figure 8.

* -- CHECK RESIDS FOR LACK OF FIT & HETEROGENOUS VARIANCE BELOW
BREAKPOINT-- *;
SYMBOL1 f=marker v=U i=none c=black;
AXIS2 label = (a=90 r=0);
PROC GPLOT DATA=PIECEFIT;
    WHERE (X <= 4.83);
    PLOT RESID*PRED=1 / frame VAXIS=AXIS2 VREF=0;
RUN;
* -- CHECK RESIDS FOR LACK OF FIT & HETEROGENOUS VARIANCE ABOVE BREAKPOINT-- *;
PROC GPLOT DATA=PIECEFIT;
    WHERE (X > 4.83);
    PLOT RESID*PRED=1 / FRAME VAXIS=AXIS2 VREF=0;
RUN;
```

Implications of assumption violations

When the residuals are not independent, then a time series analysis may be more appropriate for predicting changes in transport rate over time. When the linearity assumption is violated, then a linear model is not the best fit for the data. Violations of the normality and/or homogeneous variance assumptions result in unreliable estimates of the standard error and confidence intervals for the model parameters, but the parameter estimates themselves are unbiased (Neter and others 1990). A nonparametric method, such as bootstrapping, can be used to estimate the accuracy in the estimation of a parameter (Efron and Tibshirani 1993). Bootstrapping involves resampling from the original dataset, with replacement, in order to obtain a secondary dataset. The piecewise model is then fit to the secondary datasets and the parameter estimates (a_1, b_1, b_2, c) are retained. Using the parameter estimates from secondary datasets generated in these analysis (n=2000), nonparametric standard errors and confidence intervals can be estimated for the original piecewise regression model. If the data exhibit violations of the normality and variance assumptions as well as the independence assumption, it is up to the user to determine if they would prefer to use a time series approach to the analysis or address primarily the normality and variance issues, and realize possible bias of the MSE due to the correlation issue.

For the Little Granite Creek data, the MSE from the autoregressive model applied to the residuals did not differ substantially from the original model MSE, so we chose to ignore the modest correlation effect and focus on the lack of normality and homogeneous variance problems. Bootstrapping techniques were used to obtain confidence intervals and standard errors for the piecewise regression model (table 3). The analysis estimates the breakpoint as 4.8 $m^3 s^{-1}$ with 95 percent confidence interval ranging from 3.97 to 8.00 $m^3 s^{-1}$, which is a fairly sizable range (fig. 9, table 3). Sampling more data points at flows near

Table 3—Little Granite Creek piecewise regression parameter values with corresponding bootstrap estimates of the standard error and 95 percent confidence intervals.

Parameter	Estimate	Bootstrap standard error	95% BCa[a] Confidence intervals (lower, upper)	
a_1	-0.00223	0.01174	-0.04413	0.00076
b_1	0.00355	0.00497	0.00177	0.02104
b_2	0.10936	0.07082	0.07064	0.25879
c	4.83411	0.94901	3.96558	8.00188

[a]BCa confidence intervals are considered the better bootstrap intervals because they are bettered bias-corrected and accelerated confidence intervals (Efron and Tibshirani 1993).

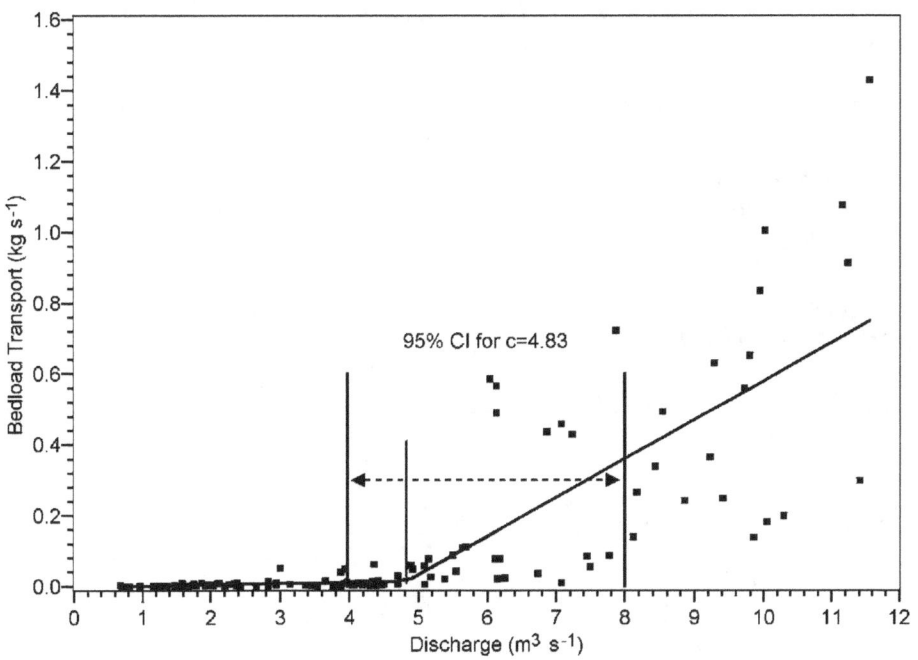

Figure 9—Piecewise regression fit between discharge and bedload transport data collected at Little Granite Creek with error bars denoting width of 95 percent confidence intervals for the estimated breakpoint.

the breakpoint value might improve the fit and confidence of the estimates. It is also important to note that this is where the variance in the data starts to rapidly increase, which also contributes to wider confidence bands. A discharge of 4.8 m^3 s^{-1} is about 81 percent of the bankfull discharge determined for this site ($Q_{1.5}$ = 5.95 m^3 s^{-1}). Ryan and others (2002, 2005) have shown that the breakpoint occurs at about 80 percent of the bankfull discharge in many gravel bed channels measured in Colorado and Wyoming. The confidence bands on this estimate are typically between 60 and 100 percent of the bankfull discharge.

Hayden Creek Example

Data from Hayden Creek near Salida, CO was collected by staff from the USFS Rocky Mountain Research Station and the Pike/San Isabel National Forest during snowmelt runoff in 1998 and 1999. This dataset has very few observations collected at higher flows, making the piecewise regression model fitting more challenging and the interpretations more difficult. Repeating the series of steps outlined for Little Granite Creek, the data for Hayden Creek are first plotted with the nonparameteric LOESS fit to estimate the value of the breakpoint (box 9). The breakpoint is visually estimated to be somewhere between 1.3 m^3 s^{-1} and 1.7 m^3 s^{-1} (fig. 10).

Box 9. Apply a nonparametric smooth to the data and generate figure 10.

```
* -- USE LOESS PROCEDURE TO GET SMOOTHED NONPARAMETRIC FIT OF DATA -- *;
PROC LOESS DATA=hayden;
    MODEL Y=X;
    ODS OUTPUT OUTPUTSTATISTICS=LOESSFIT;
RUN;
* -- PLOT DATA AND THE LOESS FIT -- *;
SYMBOL1 f=marker v=U i=none c=black;
SYMBOL2 v=none i=join line=1 c=black;
AXIS2 label = (a=90 r=0);
PROC GPLOT DATA=LOESSFIT;
    PLOT DEPVAR*X=1 PRED*X=2 / OVERLAY FRAME VAXIS=AXIS2;
RUN;
```

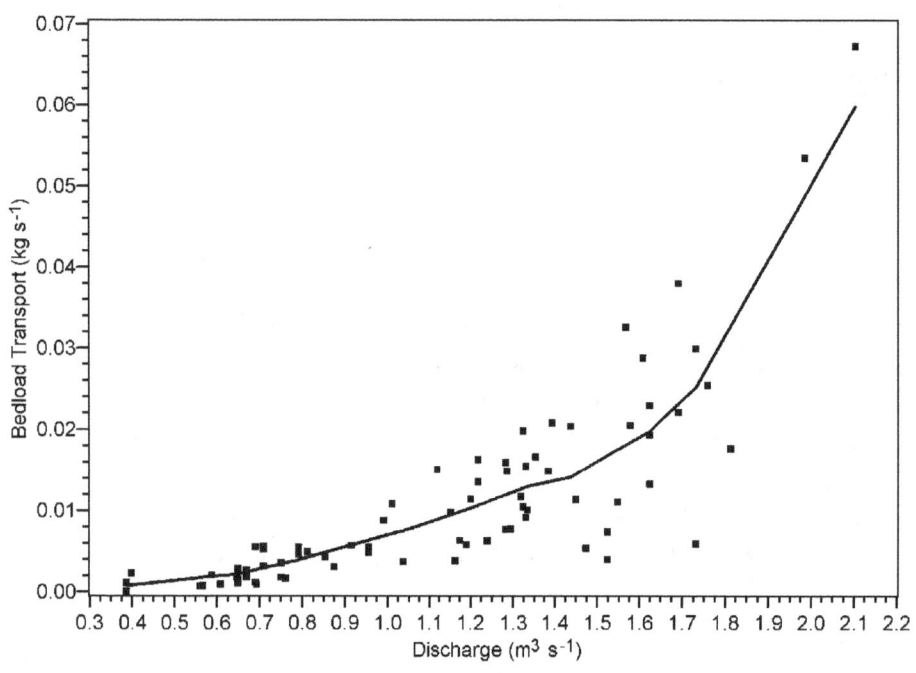

Figure 10—Loess fit between discharge and bedload transport data collected at Hayden Creek.

Next, a standard linear regression model is fit to the entire data range (fig. 11, box 10). It appears there may be a better model than the linear fit for this data.

Box 10. Apply a linear regression model to the data and generate figure 11.

```
* -- APPLY LINEAR REGRESSION MODEL TO THE DATA -- *;
PROC REG DATA=hayden;
  MODEL Y=X;
  OUTPUT OUT=LINEARFIT P=PRED;
RUN;
* -- PLOT DATA AND THE LINEAR REGRESSION FIT -- *;
SYMBOL1 f=marker v=U i=none c=black;
SYMBOL2 v=none i=join line=1 c=black;
AXIS2 label = (a=90 r=0);
PROC GPLOT DATA=LINEARFIT;
  PLOT Y*X=1 PRED*X=2 / OVERLAY FRAME VAXIS=AXIS2;
RUN;
```

Analysis of Variance

Source	DF	Sum of Squares	Mean Square	F Value	Pr > F
Model	1	0.00627	0.00627	110.95	<.0001
Error	74	0.00418	0.00005653		
Corrected Total	75	0.01046			

Root MSE	0.00752	R-Square	0.5999
Dependent Mean	0.01097	Adj R-Sq	0.5945
Coeff Var	68.52498		

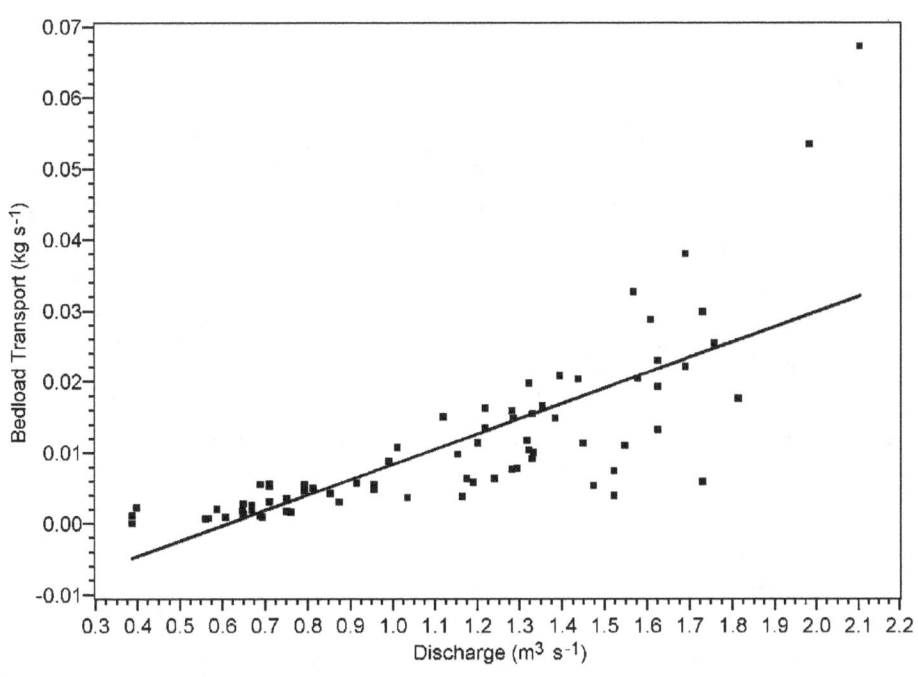

Figure 11—Linear fit between discharge and bedload transport data collected at Hayden Creek.

With an estimated breakpoint between 1.3 and 1.7 m³ s⁻¹, the initial starting parameters are obtained for models where the breakpoint was 1.3, 1.5 (half-way), and 1.7. The following code is used to obtain starting parameters estimates for a breakpoint at 1.5 (fig. 12, box 11). The estimated parameters used in the analysis are shown table 4.

Box 11. Apply two linear regression models to the data and generate figure 12.

```
* -- APPLY LINEAR REG MODEL TO DATA BELOW ESTIMATED BREAKPOINT -- *;
PROC REG DATA=hayden;
   MODEL Y=X;
   OUTPUT OUT=FITBELOW P=PREDBELOW;
   WHERE X <= 1.5;
RUN;
* -- APPLY LINEAR REG MODEL TO DATA ABOVE ESTIMATED BREAKPOINT -- *;
PROC REG DATA=hayden;
   MODEL Y=X;
   OUTPUT OUT=FITABOVE P=PREDABOVE;
   WHERE X > 1.5;
RUN;
* -- COMBINE DATASETS -- *;
DATA FITBOTH;
   SET FITBELOW FITABOVE;
RUN;
* -- PLOT DATA AND THE TWO LINEAR REGRESSION FITS -- *;
SYMBOL1 f=marker v=U i=none c=black;
SYMBOL2 v=none i=join line=1 c=black;
AXIS2 label = (a=90 r=0);
PROC GPLOT DATA=FITBOTH;
   PLOT Y*X=1 PREDBELOW*X=2 PREDABOVE*X=2 / OVERLAY FRAME VAXIS=AXIS2;
RUN;
```

Linear Fit **Below** Estimated Breakpoint=1.5

Variable	Label	DF	Parameter Estimate	Standard Error	t Value	Pr > |t|
Intercept	Intercept	1	-0.00675	0.00137	-4.92	<.0001
X	Discharge (cubic meters/sec)	1	0.01435	0.00136	10.57	<.0001

Linear Fit **At and Above** Estimated Breakpoint=1.5

Variable	Label	DF	Parameter Estimate	Standard Error	t Value	Pr > |t|
Intercept	Intercept	1	-0.11531	0.02823	-4.09	0.0010
X	Discharge (cubic meters/sec)	1	0.08285	0.01663	4.98	0.0002

Using these parameters, the piecewise regression model is fit with PROC NLIN procedure (fig. 13, box 12).

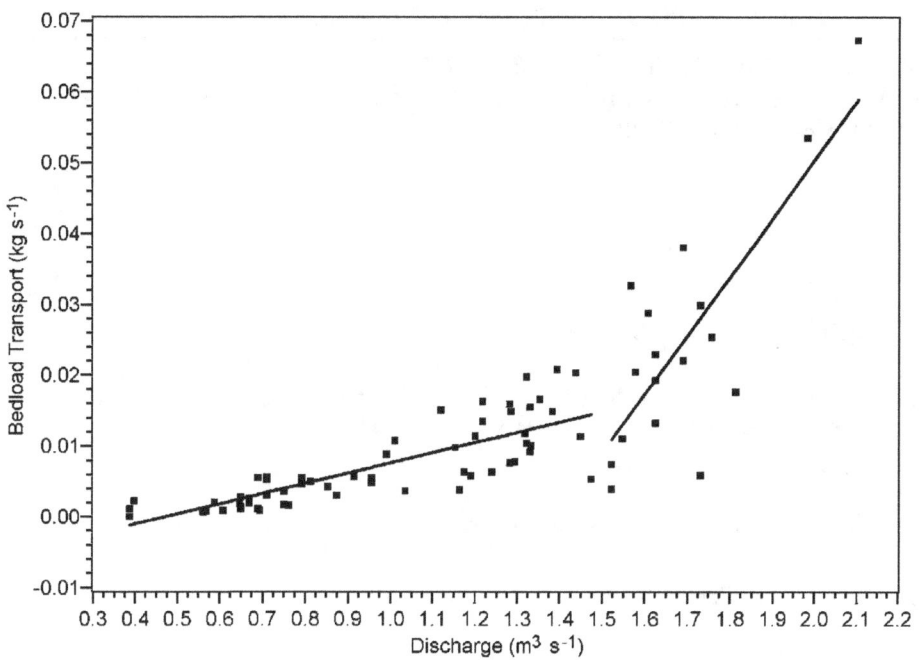

Figure 12—Two estimates of linear fits between discharge and bedload transport below and above an estimated breakpoint of 1.5. Data are from Hayden Creek.

Table 4—Estimated piecewise regression starting parameters for Hayden Creek with an estimated breakpoint at 1.5.

Parameter	Estimated starting parameter	How obtained
a_1	-0.00675	Intercept of linear fit to data **below** estimated breakpoint.
b_1	0.01435	Slope of linear fit to data **below** estimated breakpoint.
b_2	0.08285	Slope of linear fit to data **above** estimated breakpoint.
c	1.5	Estimated breakpoint from LOESS plot.

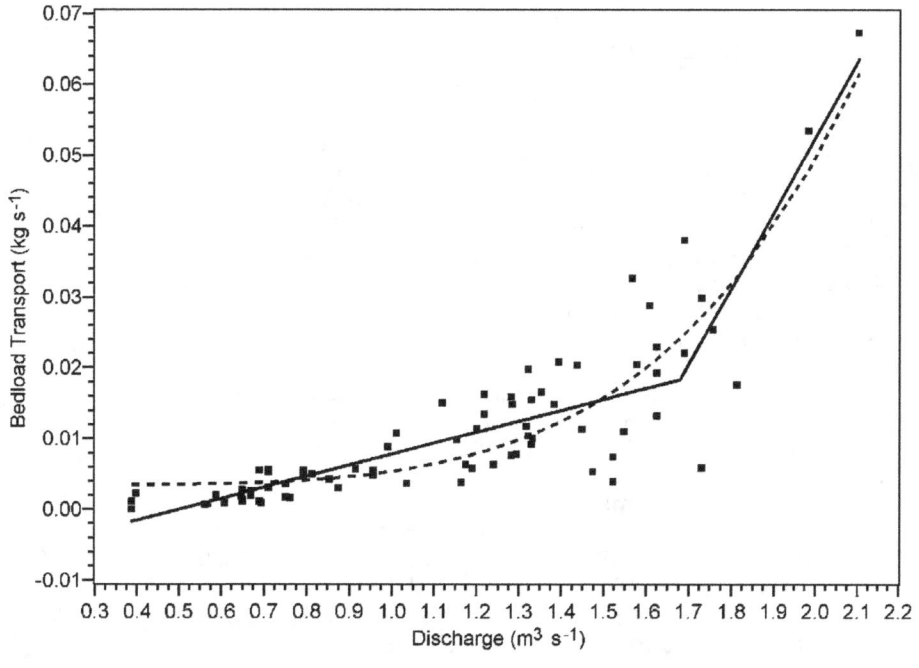

Figure 13—Piecewise regression and power fit between discharge and bedload transport data collected at Hayden Creek.

Box 12. Apply a piecewise and power model to the data and generate figure 13.

```
* -- FIT THE PIECEWISE MODEL USING NONLINEAR PROCEDURE -- *;
PROC NLIN DATA=hayden MAXITER=1000 METHOD=MARQUARDT;
   PARMS a1=-0.00675 b1=0.01435 c=1.5 b2=0.08285;
   Xpart = a1 + b1*X;
   IF (X > c) THEN DO;
      Xpart = a1 + c*(b1-b2) + b2*X;
      end;
   MODEL Y = Xpart;
   OUTPUT OUT=PIECEFIT R=RESID P=PRED;
RUN;
* -- FIT THE POWER MODEL (FOR COMPARISON) USING NONLINEAR PROCEDURE -- *;
PROC NLIN DATA=hayden MAXITER=1000 METHOD=MARQUARDT;
   PARMS a1=0.01 b1=0.01 b2=1.0;
   MODEL Y = a1 + b1*X**b2;
   OUTPUT OUT=POWERFIT R=PWR_RESID P=PWR_PRED;
RUN;
* -- COMBINE OUTPUT FROM BOTH MODELS -- *;
DATA ALL;
   SET PIECEFIT POWERFIT;
RUN;
* -- PLOT DATA, PIECEWISE REGRESSION FIT, AND POWER MODEL FIT -- *;
SYMBOL1 f=marker v=U i=none c=black;
SYMBOL2 v=none i=join line=1 w=3 c=black;
SYMBOL3 v=none i=join line=2 w=3 c=black;
AXIS2 label = (a=90 r=0);
PROC GPLOT DATA=ALL;
   PLOT Y*X=1 PRED*X=2 PWR_PRED*X=3 / OVERLAY FRAME VAXIS=AXIS2;
RUN;
```

Hayden Creek
Piecewise Regression Fit
The NLIN Procedure
Dependent Variable y
Method: Marquardt

Iterative Phase

Iter	a1	b1	c	b2	Sum of Squares
0	-0.00675	0.0144	1.5000	0.0829	0.00288
1	-0.00675	0.0144	1.5848	0.0828	0.00240
2	-0.00678	0.0144	1.6104	0.0882	0.00238
3	-0.00753	0.0153	1.6504	0.0962	0.00232
4	-0.00772	0.0155	1.6842	0.1067	0.00230
5	-0.00772	0.0155	1.6804	0.1067	0.00230

NOTE: Convergence criterion met.

Source	DF	Sum of Squares	Mean Square	Approx F Value	Pr > F
Model	3	0.00816	0.00272	85.24	<.0001
Error	72	0.00230	0.000032		
Corrected Total	75	0.0105			

Parameter	Estimate	Approx Std Error	Approximate 95% Confidence Limits	
a1	-0.00772	0.00207	-0.0118	-0.00360
b1	0.0155	0.00188	0.0118	0.0193
c	1.6804	0.0336	1.6134	1.7475
b2	0.1067	0.0141	0.0785	0.1348

The model converged with a breakpoint at 1.68 and an MSE of 0.000032 (box 12). If we repeat the above analyses estimating a breakpoint at 1.3, it produces the same model as a starting breakpoint of 1.5. However, using a starting value of 1.7 for the breakpoint, a converging model with a breakpoint at 1.81 (MSE=0.000029) results. This MSE is smaller, but there are then only three data points above this breakpoint, which doesn't produce a viable model. It is clear at this point there are two observations in the dataset that are potential outliers. The effects of these points will be investigated later in the tutorial.

Comparing the mean squared errors of the linear (fig. 11), power (fig. 13), and piecewise regression (fig. 13) models it is apparent the linear model is not the best model. The power and piecewise regression model have very similar MSEs (table 5).

Table 5—Model standard errors for the linear, power, and piecewise regression models for Hayden Creek.

Least squares model	Model standard error
Linear: $y = a_1 + b_1 x$	0.000057
Power: $y = a_1 + b_1 x^{b2}$	0.000033
Piecewise	0.000032

Next, the assumptions of an ordinary least squares model are tested along with an examination of the dependence of the residuals (fig. 14, box 13).

Box 13. Check residuals for independence by generating figure 14.

```
* -- SORT THE DATA BY TIME -- *;
PROC SORT DATA=PIECEFIT;
   BY date;
RUN;
* -- ADD A DUMMY TIME VARIABLE TO MAKE PLOTTING EASIER -- *;
DATA PIECEFIT;
   RETAIN TIME 0;
   SET PIECEFIT;
   TIME = TIME + 1;
RUN;
* -- PLOT THE RESIDUALS OVER TIME IN ORDER TO CHECK FOR INDEPENDENCE -- *;
SYMBOL1 f=marker v=U i=join c=black;
AXIS2 label = (a=90 r=0);
PROC GPLOT DATA=PIECEFIT;
   PLOT X*TIME=1 / FRAME VAXIS=AXIS2;
RUN;
```

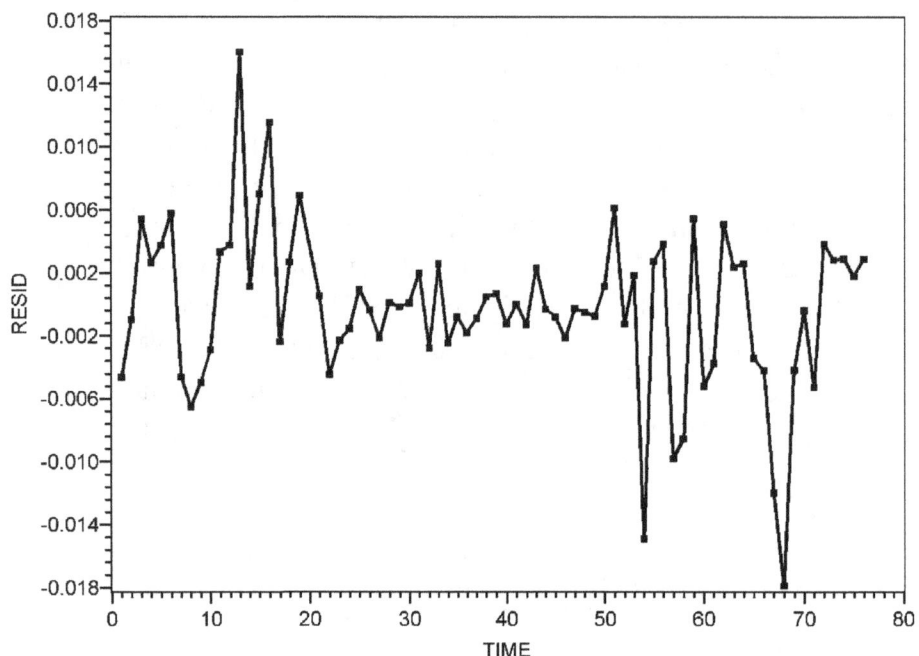

Figure 14—Piecewise regression residuals for Hayden Creek plotted sequentially to check for independence.

It appears the residuals may be correlated, so we model the residuals using an autoregressive variance structure (box 14). The nonlinear least squares MSE of 0.000032 is not substantially different from the MSE that takes correlation into account (0.000030), so we conclude that the original MSE adequately represents the model.

Box 14. Apply an autoregressive model to the residuals.

```
*-- SORT THE DATA BY TIME -- *;
PROC SORT DATA=PIECEFIT;
   BY date;
RUN;
* -- MODEL THE RESIDUALS AS AN AR(1) -- *;
PROC MIXED DATA=PIECEFIT;
   MODEL RESID=;
   REPEATED / SUBJECT=year TYPE=AR(1);
RUN;
```

Hayden Creek
GET MSE ADJUSTED FOR CORRELATION

Convergence criteria met.

Covariance Parameter Estimates

Cov Parm	Subject	Estimate	Standard Error	Z Value	Pr Z	Alpha	Lower	Upper
AR(1)	YEAR	0.2841	0.1090	2.61	0.0091	0.05	0.07052	0.4977
Residual		0.000030	5.271E-6	5.72	<.0001	0.05	0.000022	0.000044

Examining the residuals for normality (box 15), we cannot reject the assumption of normality of the data above the breakpoint (fig. 15b). Assuming an alpha of 0.05, the Shapiro-Wilk test for the data below the breakpoint have a borderline p-value of 0.0438 (fig 15a). The other normality tests have p-values greater than 0.05 so we conclude the residuals for both segments appear to be normal.

Box 15. Check residuals for normality and generate figure 15.

```
* -- CHECK RESIDUALS FOR NORMALITY BELOW THE BREAKPOINT -- *;
SYMBOL1 f=marker v=U i=none c=black;
PROC UNIVARIATE DATA=PIECEFIT NORMAL;
   WHERE (X <= 1.68);
   VAR RESID;
   QQPLOT RESID / NORMAL(MU=EST SIGMA=EST);
RUN;
* -- CHECK RESIDUALS FOR NORMALITY ABOVE THE BREAKPOINT -- *;
PROC UNIVARIATE DATA=PIECEFIT NORMAL;
   WHERE (X > 1.68);
   VAR RESID;
   QQPLOT RESID / NORMAL(MU=EST SIGMA=EST);
RUN;
```

Tests for Normality
Checking for Normality Below the Breakpoint

Test	--------Statistic--------		----------p Value----------	
Shapiro-Wilk	W	0.963472	Pr < W	0.0438
Kolmogorov-Smirnov	D	0.080942	Pr > D	>0.1500
Cramer-von Mises	W-Sq	0.087773	Pr > W-Sq	0.1652
Anderson-Darling	A-Sq	0.608608	Pr > A-Sq	0.1110

Tests for Normality
Checking for Normality Above the Breakpoint

Test	--------Statistic--------		----------p Value----------	
Shapiro-Wilk	W	0.917241	Pr < W	0.4079
Kolmogorov-Smirnov	D	0.215632	Pr > D	>0.1500
Cramer-von Mises	W-Sq	0.079648	Pr > W-Sq	0.1875
Anderson-Darling	A-Sq	0.427314	Pr > A-Sq	0.2364

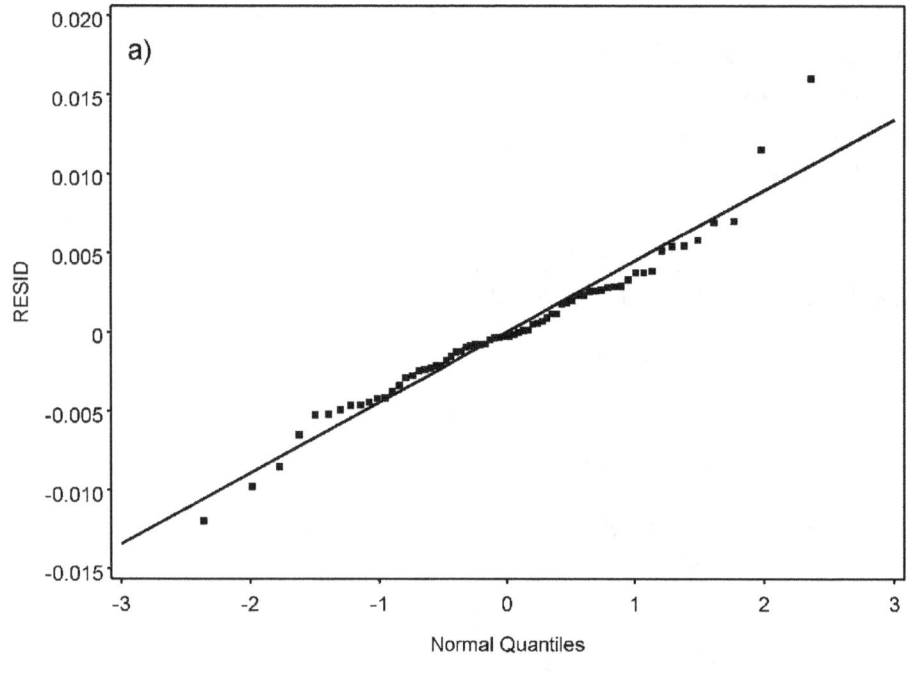

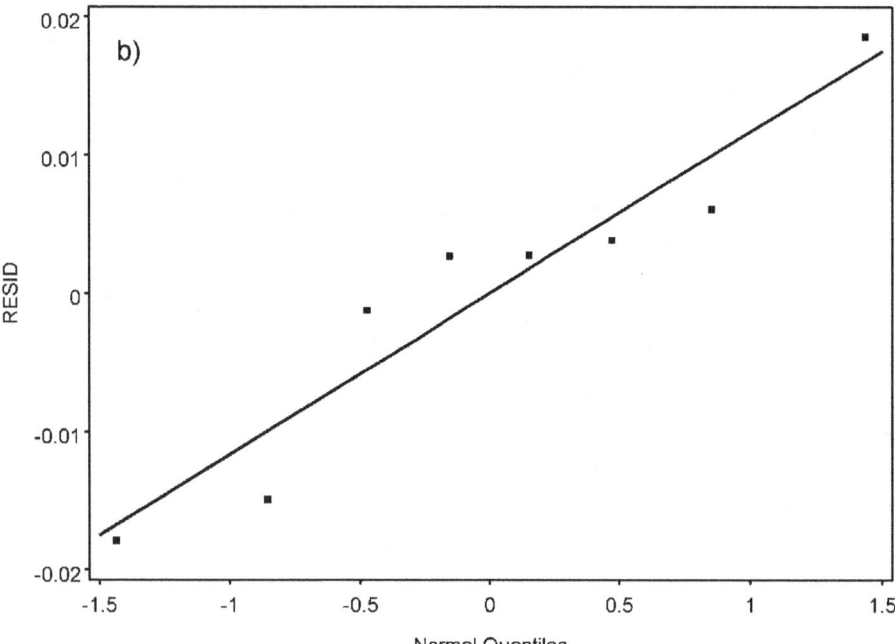

Figure 15—QQ-plots for Hayden Creek piecewise regression residuals for curve fits (a) below and (b) above the breakpoint.

Checking the residuals for homogeneous variance and linearity (box 16), we find that the linearity of the data is not in question because half the data are above and below the line (fig. 16 a, b). However, the variance is not homogeneous. Since the residuals do not exhibit homogeneous variance, we use bootstrapping methods to obtain appropriate standard errors and confidence intervals for the parameter estimates (a_1, b_1, b_2, c) in the piecewise regression model (fig. 17, table 6).

```
*-- CHECK RESIDS FOR LACK OF FIT & HETEROGENOUS VARIANCE BELOW BREAKPOINT
-- *;
SYMBOL1 f=marker v=U i=none c=black;
AXIS2 label = (a=90 r=0);
PROC GPLOT DATA=PIECEFIT;
   WHERE (X <= 1.68);
   PLOT RESID*PRED=1 / frame VAXIS=AXIS2 VREF=0;
RUN;
*-- CHECK RESIDS FOR LACK OF FIT & HETEROGENOUS VARIANCE ABOVE BREAKPOINT -- *;
PROC GPLOT DATA=PIECEFIT;
   WHERE (X > 1.68);
   PLOT RESID*PRED=1 / FRAME VAXIS=AXIS2 VREF=0;
RUN;
```

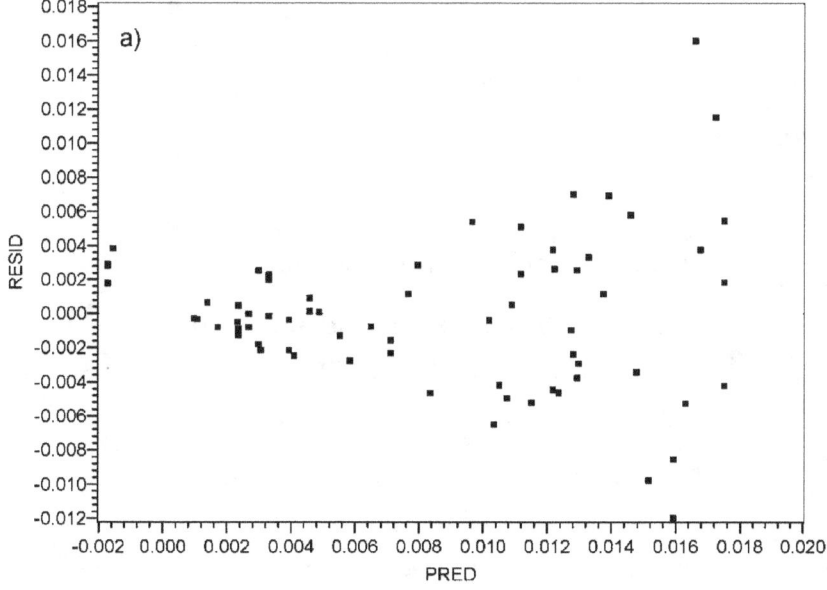

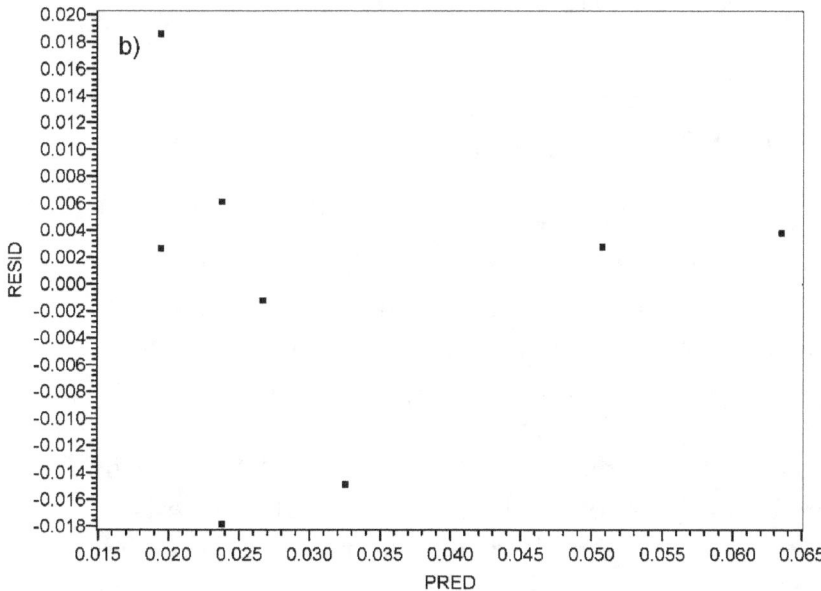

Figure 16—Hayden Creek piecewise regression residuals and predicted values (a) below and (b) above the breakpoint.

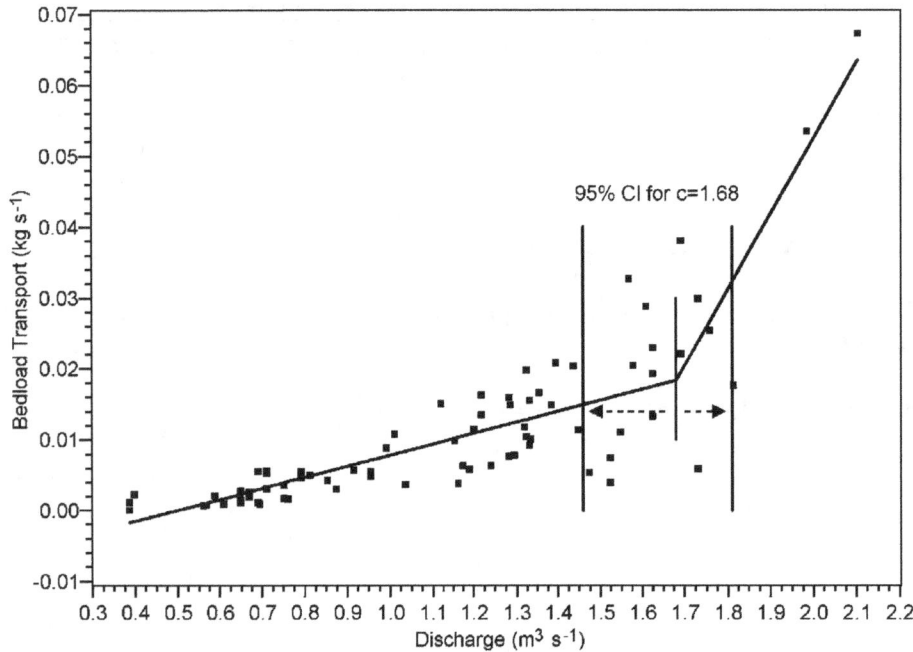

Figure 17—Piecewise regression fit between discharge and bedload transport data collected at Hayden Creek with error bars denoting width of 95 percent confidence intervals for the estimated breakpoint.

Table 6—Hayden Creek piecewise regression parameter estimates with corresponding bootstrap estimates of the standard error and 95 percent confidence intervals.

Parameter	Estimate	Bootstrap standard error	95% BCa[1] Confidence intervals (lower, upper)	
a_1	-0.0077	0.00167	-0.01042	-0.00376
b_1	0.0155	0.00211	0.01052	0.01873
b_2	0.1067	0.02891	0.02983	0.17383
c	1.6804	0.10540	1.46113	1.80788

[1]BCa confidence intervals are considered the better bootstrap intervals because they are bettered bias-corrected and accelerated confidence intervals (Efron and Tibshirani 1993).

Potential Outliers

An assessment of potential outliers is important in any analysis. When dealing with measurements of bedload transport, it is common to have outlying data points. However, while a data point should not be removed simply because it is an outlier, it is important to know how these points affect the model fit. Fitting methods such as least absolute deviations (LAD) or iteratively reweighted least squares (IRLS) decrease the affect of outliers on the model fit. For consistency, we use standard least squares to fit the piecewise regression model, but also assess the affect of outliers on the location of the breakpoint. The piecewise model without these extraneous data points is fit and compared against the

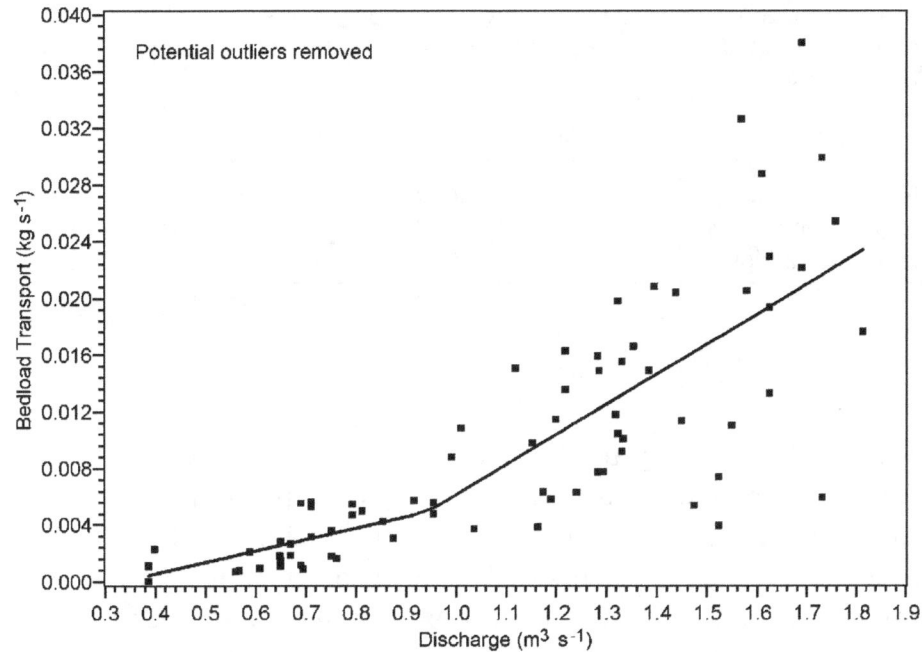

Figure 18—Piecewise regression fit between discharge versus bedload transport data collected at Hayden Creek, with the removal of two high flow observations.

original fit. When the differences are substantial, the user must determine if the outlying data points should be left in the model or removed for scientific or procedural reasons.

In the Hayden Creek example, two high flow points appear to be very influential observations in fitting the models. If we remove these points and refit the piecewise regression model, the breakpoint moves from 1.68 to 1.0 (fig. 18), providing a very different answer from the original. Additional evidence hints that piecewise model may not be an appropriate model to use in the absence of these data points. For instance, there is only a slight change in slope between the upper and lower modeled segments with the outlying points removed, implying that there may be only one linear segment. Moreover, the calculated MSE for the linear model is not substantially different from the piecewise or power model (table 7), suggesting that a linear fit without these points is as appropriate for these data as the more complex models. Based on this evidence, the range of data in figure 18 likely represents phase I transport and the two outlying data points characterize a limited sampling of phase II transport. More measurements at higher flows would have been beneficial for this data set and demonstrates the importance of obtaining data from a wide range of flows. Furthermore, there is no reason to believe these data points are invalid (in other words there was no instrument or procedural failure) and therefore, we conclude that the original model with all of the data included is the better model for Hayden Creek.

Table 7—Model standard errors for the linear, power, and piecewise regression models for Hayden Creek—with the removal of the two high flow observations.

Least squares model	Model standard error
Linear—w/out 2 high flows	0.000028
Power—w/out 2 high flows	0.000027
Piecewise—w/out 2 high flows	0.000028

Guidelines

The number of data points necessary to obtain a good fit using piecewise linear regression depends on a number of factors. Given the inherent variability common in bedload data, a relatively large number of samples from a wide flow range are typically needed to define the piecewise (as well as other) models. In order to examine how sample size can affect the fitting of a piecewise linear regression model, smaller datasets were generated from their larger counterparts by randomly sampling data points and attempting to fit a piecewise regression model. Data from nine different sites (table 8) were used in these comparisons: East St. Louis Creek, Little Granite Creek, Lower Fool Creek, St. Louis Creek Sites 1-5, and St. Louis Creek Site 4a (Ryan and others 2002, 2005). The piecewise regression models, or "reference models," against which we compare the subsampling results are shown in figure 19 (see also Appendix B). These reference models are considered the "true" piecewise linear regression models because the model was generated using the entire dataset. Data from most of these sites had normality and/or homogeneous variance problems, as is typical with this type of data, so bootstrapping methods were used to develop 95 percent confidence intervals for the parameter estimates.

Table 8—Sites used in subsampling analysis and corresponding number of observations each dataset contains.

Site	Number of observations
East St. Louis Creek	109
Little Granite Creek	123
Lower Fool Creek	95
St. Louis Creek Site 1	92
St. Louis Creek Site 2	118
St. Louis Creek Site 3	107
St. Louis Creek Site 4	127
St. Louis Creek Site 4a	104
St. Louis Creek Site 5	94

Bootstrap resampling methods were used to generate datasets (subsamples) containing 20, 30, 40, 60, 80, and 100 data points (when n > 100) selected from the original dataset. In order to force each subsample to contain data from the entire range of flow, the original data were grouped into four different bins based on flow level relative to the bankfull discharge (table 9). For each site and subsample size, 1000 resampled datasets were generated by randomly sampling with replacement from each of the four bins. The first bin represented 20 percent of the data, so 20 percent of each newly generated dataset were random samples from bin one. The second bin represented 25 percent of the data, so 25 percent of each newly generated dataset were random samples from bin two. The same scheme was used for bins three and four. Once the subsample datasets were generated, a piecewise linear regression model was fit, and if the model converged, bootstrap methods were used to obtain confidence intervals for the parameters and model standard error (SE). Models that failed to converge were eliminated.

Table 9—Description of bins where the data fell and the average percentage of data contained in each bin (BF = bankfull).

Bin #	Data contained within bin	% of Data in each bin
1	$0 <= X <= 1/3*BF$	20%
2	$1/3*BF < X <= 2/3*BF$	25%
3	$2/3*BF < X <= BF$	25%
4	$X > BF$	30%

The primary result of interest in a piecewise linear regression model using bedload data is the estimate of the breakpoint. In order to estimate the sample size that will provide a breakpoint that is not substantially different from the "reference" model breakpoint, we determined how many of the converging models had a breakpoint within the 95 percent bootstrap confidence intervals of the "reference" model. In other words, how many of the subsampled datasets converged with a breakpoint estimate that was not substantially different from that of the full model. Similarly, we determined how often both the subsample breakpoint and model SE were within the acceptable range of the "reference" model (table 10).

Table 10—Average percentage of subsamples with 1) breakpoint inside the 95% CIs of the "reference" breakpoint, and 2) breakpoint and model SE within the 95% corresponding "reference" CIs.

Subsample size	Average % inside CI for c_1	Average % inside CI for c_1 and CI for model SE
20	66	36
30	75	49
40	81	60
60	88	72
80	92	79
100	93	82

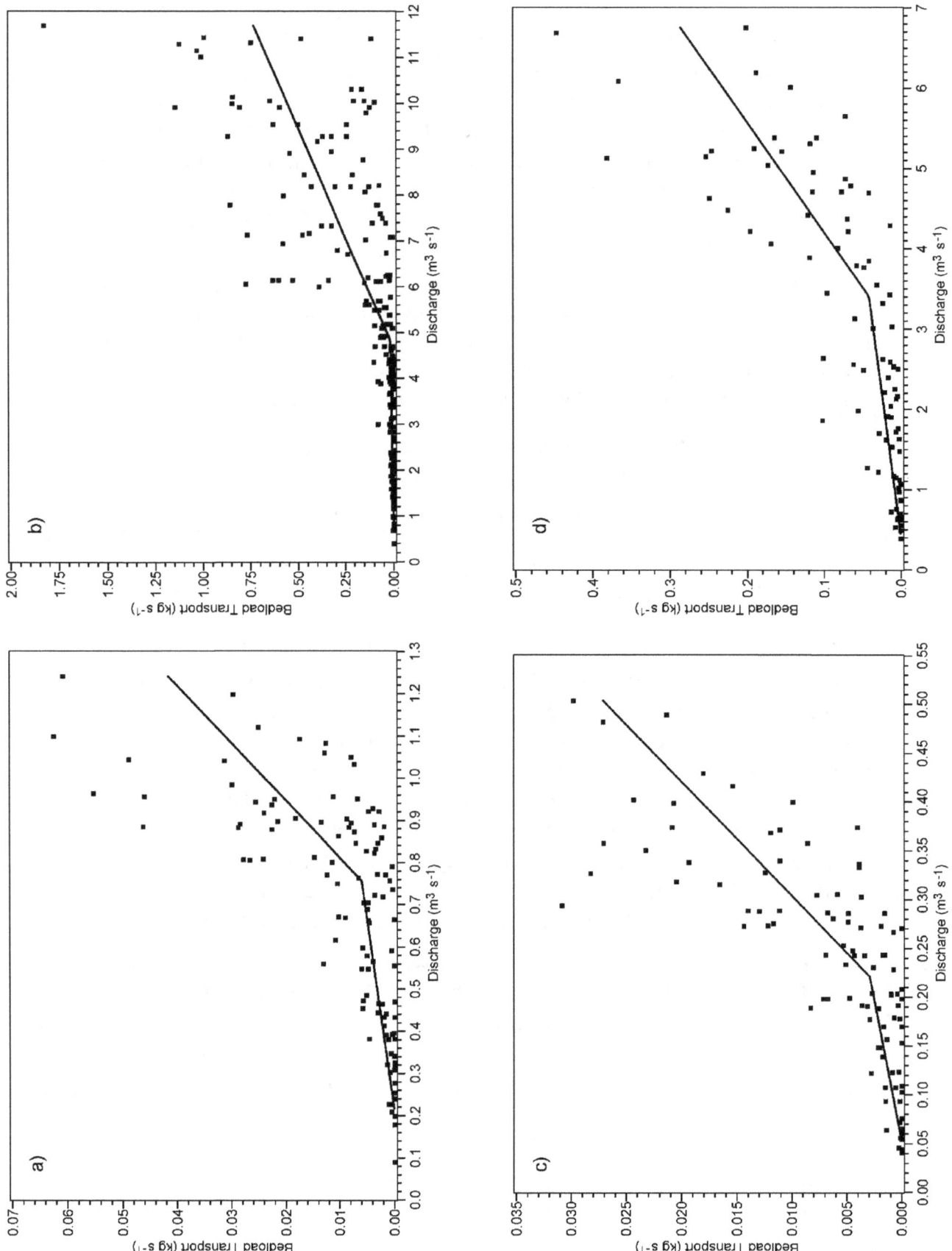

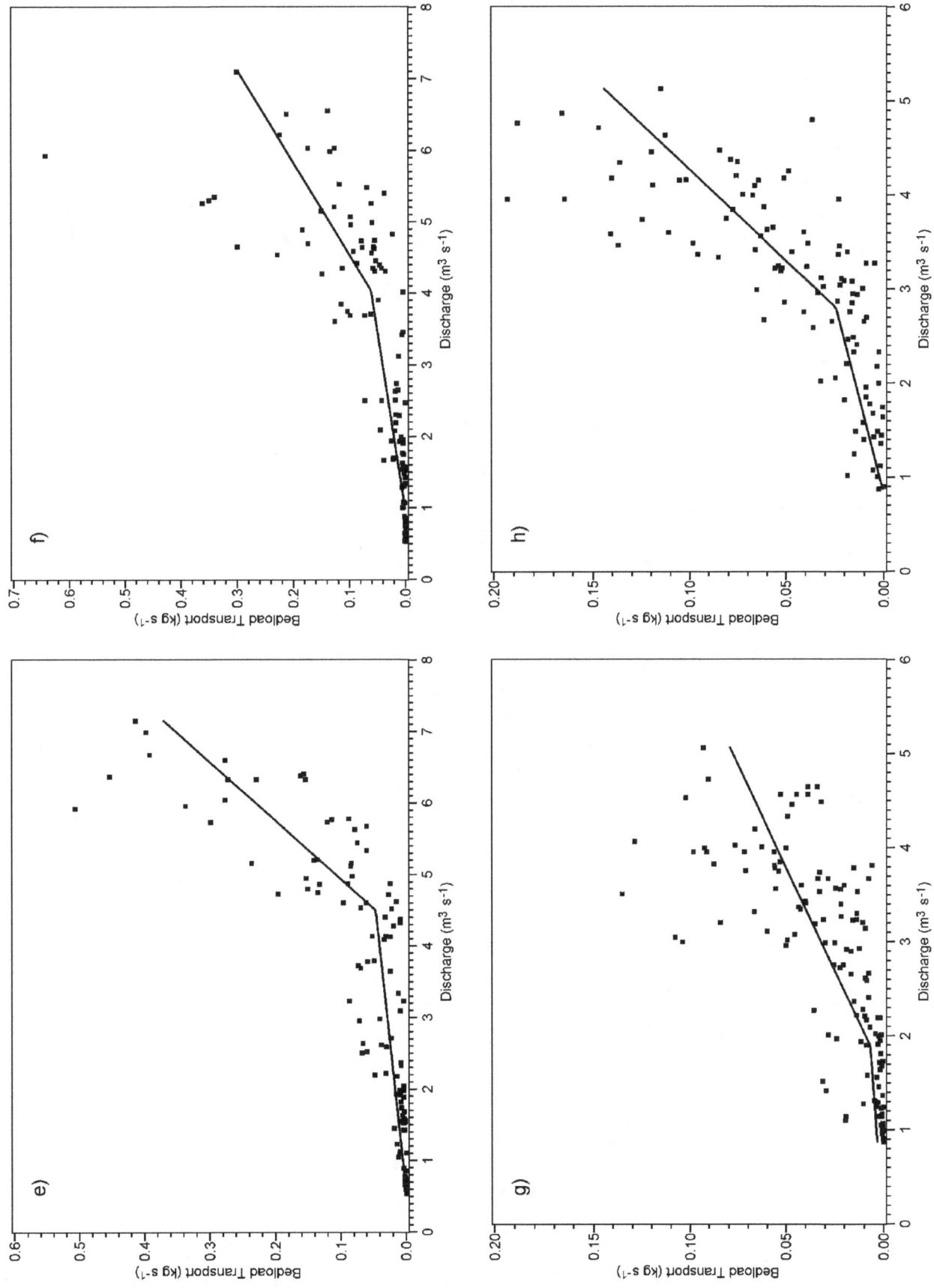

Figure 19—Piecewise regression fit for discharge vs. bedload transport at (a) East St. Louis Creek, (b) Little Granite Creek, (c) Fool Creek, (d) St. Louis Creek Site 1, (e) St. Louis Creek Site 2, (f) St. Louis Creek Site 3; (g) St. Louis Creek Site 4, (h) St. Louis Creek Site 4a, and (i) St. Louis Creek Site 5.

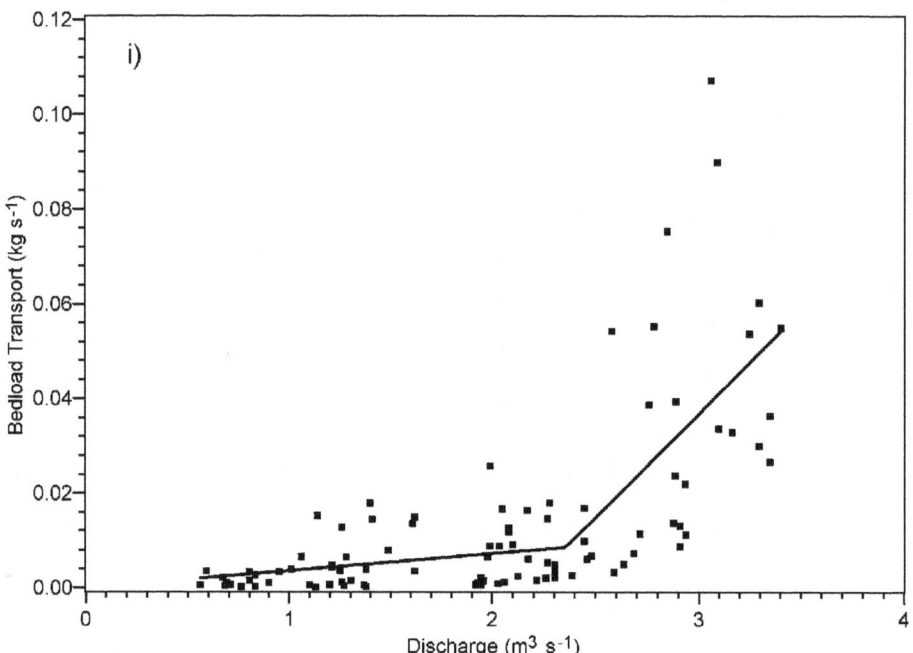

Figure 19i—*continued.*

Models developed from subsamples of size 20 had breakpoints within the confidence intervals 66 percent of the time. Requiring the subsamples to have both a breakpoint and model SE within the 95 percent confidence intervals of the "reference" model dropped the percentage to 36 percent (table 10). Notably, there is marked improvement in the percentages of subsamples with a breakpoint and model SE within the acceptable range at sample size 40. In practice, we observed that datasets containing fewer than 40 data points often have convergence problems, primarily because it is difficult to adequately define transport rates over sub-ranges of flows using fewer measurements. Our results here concur with those observations pertaining to minimum sample size needed to adequately define a breakpoint for bedload data. The benefits of increasing the sample size are not as substantial when the subsample size increases from 60 to 80 data points. Samples of size 60 and 80, when obtained by sampling across the entire range of data, resulted in models with a breakpoint within the 95 percent confidence interval of the "true" breakpoint 88 to 92 percent of the time. Subsamples with both a breakpoint and model SE within the acceptable range of the reference model occurred 72 to 79 percent of the time with samples of size 60 and 80. These results indicate that collecting more than 80 bedload samples does not greatly improve the estimate of the "true" breakpoint. Hence, the cost of obtaining samples where $n>80$, may not outweigh the benefits in terms of model explanation, as long as the entire flow regime is sampled.

Summary

In this tutorial, we demonstrated the application of piecewise linear regression to bedload data for defining a breakpoint, presumed to represent a shift in phase of transport, so that the reader may perform similar analyses. General statistical theory behind piecewise regression and its procedural approaches were presented, including two examples applied to bedload data from sites in Wyoming and Colorado. The results from a number of additional bedload datasets from St. Louis Creek watershed near Fraser, Colorado were provided to show the range of estimated values and confidence limits on the breakpoint that the analysis provides. Given the inherent variability common in bedload data, a relatively large number of samples from a wide range of flows is needed to define the piecewise regression model. We concluded from a subsampling exercise that a minimum of 40 samples of total bedload transport be obtained for performing the piecewise regression analysis. However, using more than 80 bedload samples did not greatly improve the model's ability to estimate the "actual" breakpoint. Identification and resolution of common problems encountered in bedload datasets, such as the influence of outliers and other statistical issues, were also addressed. Data points should not be removed simply because they lie outside of the range of other data, but it is important to know how these points affect the model fit and then judge whether they should be retained. Finally, the code for generating the analysis in SAS provided in bold text in the document has been made available online at the following URL: http://stream. fs.fed.us/publications/software.html.

References

Andrews, E.D. 1984. Bed-material entrainment and hydraulic geometry of gravel-bed rivers in Colorado. Geological Society of America Bulletin. 95: 371-378.

Andrews, E.D.; Nankervis, J.M. 1995. Effective discharge and the design of channel maintenance flows for gravel-bed rivers. In: Costa, J.E.; Miller, A.J.; Potter, K.W.; Wilcock, P.R. eds Natural and Anthropogenic Influences in Fluvial Geomorphology: The Wolman Volume; Geophysical Monograph 89. Washington, DC: American Geophysical Union: 151-164.

Bates, D. M.; Watts, D.G. 1988. Nonlinear Regression Analysis and Its Applications (section 3.10). New York: Wiley. 365 p.

Bunte, K.; Abt, S.R.; Potyondy, J.P.; Ryan, S.E. 2004. Measurement of coarse gravel and cobble transport using a portable bedload trap. Journal of Hydraulic Engineering. 130(9): 879-893.

Efron, B.; Tibshirani, R.J. 1993. An Introduction to the Bootstrap. New York: Chapman and Hill. 436 p.

Emmett, W.W. 1976. Bedload transport in two large, gravel-bed rivers, Idaho and Washington. In: Third Federal Inter-agency Sedimentation Conference: Proceedings; 1976 March 22-25; Denver, CO. 4: 101-114.

Gomez, B.; Naff, R.L.; Hubbell, D.W. 1989. Temporal variations in bedload transport rates associated with the migration of bedforms. Earth Surface Processes and Landforms. 14: 135-156.

Gomez, B.; Hubbell, D.W.; Stevens, H.H. 1990. At-a-point bedload sampling in the presence of dunes. Water Resources Research. 26: 2717-2931.

Jackson, W.L.; Beschta, R.L. 1982. A model of two-phase bedload transport in an Oregon Coast Range stream. Earth Surface Processes and Landforms. 7: 517-527.

Lisle, T.E. 1995. Particle size variations between bed load and bed material in natural gravel bed channels. Water Resources Research. 31(4): 1107-1118.

Neter, J.; Wasserman, W.; Kutner, M.H. 1990. Applied Linear Statistical Models, 3rd ed. Burr Ridge, IL: Irwin. 1181 p.

Paola, C.; Seal, R. 1995. Grain size patchiness as a cause of selective deposition and downstream fining. Water Resources Research. 31(5): 1395-1407.

Parker, G. 1979. Hydraulic geometry of active gravel rivers. Journal of the Hydraulics Division, American Society of Civil Engineers. 105(HY9): 1185-1201.

Parker, G.; Klingeman, P.C. 1982. On why gravel bed streams are paved. Water Resources Research. 18: 1409-1423.

Reid, I.; Frostick, L.E. 1986. Dynamics of bedload transport in Turkey Brook, a coarse grained alluvial channel. Earth Surface Processes and Landforms. 11: 143-155.

Ryan, S.E.; Emmett, W.W. 2002. The nature of flow and sediment movement at Little Granite Creek near Bondurant, Wyoming. Gen. Tech. Rep. RMRS-GTR-90. Ogden, UT: U.S. Department of Agriculture, Forest Service, Rocky Mountain Research Station. 48 p.

Ryan, S.E.; Porth, L.S.; Troendle, C.A. 2002. Defining phases of bedload transport using piecewise regression. Earth Surface Processes and Landforms. 27: 971-990.

Ryan, S.E.; Porth, L.S.; Troendle, C.A. 2005. Coarse sediment transport in mountain streams in Colorado and Wyoming, USA. Earth Surface Processes and Landforms. 30: 269-288.

SAS Institute Inc. 2004. SAS/STAT 9.1 User's Guide. Cary, NC: SAS Institute Inc.

Schmidt, L.J.; Potyondy, J.P. 2004. Quantifying channel maintenance instream flows: an approach for gravel-bed streams in the Western United States. Gen. Tech. Rep. RMRS-GTR-128. Fort Collins, CO: U.S. Department of Agriculture, Forest Service, Rocky Mountain Research Station. 33 p.

Whiting, P.J.; Dietrich, W.E.; Leopold, L.B.; Drake, T.G.; Shreve, R.L. 1988. Bedload sheets in heterogeneous sediment. Geology. 16: 105-108.

Whiting, P.J.; Stamm, J.F.; Moog, D.B.; Orndorff, R.L. 1999. Sediment-transporting flows in headwater streams. Geological Society of America Bulletin. 111(3): 450-466.

Appendix A—Little Granite Creek example dataset (x=Discharge in m³ s⁻¹, and y=Bedload Transport in kg s⁻¹).

Date	x	y	Date	x	y	Date	x	y
05/08/1985	3.936	0.0498	05/10/1990	1.954	0.0054	05/28/1993	6.117	0.0779
05/15/1985	2.945	0.0093	05/18/1990	1.558	0.0006	05/28/1993	6.740	0.0365
05/25/1985	3.653	0.0165	05/25/1990	2.039	0.0024	06/06/1993	4.390	0.0018
05/30/1985	2.832	0.0131	05/31/1990	2.266	0.0056	06/07/1993	4.333	0.0129
06/05/1985	1.926	0.0036	06/05/1990	2.039	0.0062	06/08/1993	3.880	0.0012
06/13/1985	1.586	0.0097	06/14/1990	1.784	0.0025	06/08/1993	3.795	0.0011
06/19/1985	1.246	0.0010	06/20/1990	1.728	0.0034	06/09/1993	3.767	0.0008
06/27/1985	0.821	0.0001	06/28/1990	1.473	0.0035	06/09/1993	3.540	0.0008
07/02/1985	0.708	0.0002	07/05/1990	0.963	0.0009	05/20/1997	7.878	0.7226
07/11/1985	0.680	0.0042	05/21/1991	2.662	0.0005	05/21/1997	8.174	0.2658
05/14/1986	2.011	0.0066	05/21/1991	2.662	0.0013	05/21/1997	9.799	0.6520
05/28/1986	8.439	0.3402	05/29/1991	2.832	0.0006	05/22/1997	8.546	0.4945
06/03/1986	11.413	0.2992	06/01/1991	2.436	0.0008	05/22/1997	9.232	0.3654
06/12/1986	7.080	0.0110	06/01/1991	2.436	0.0007	05/28/1997	6.186	0.0779
06/18/1986	5.098	0.0060	06/01/1991	2.379	0.0018	05/29/1997	6.868	0.4379
06/26/1986	2.945	0.0047	06/03/1991	3.143	0.0066	05/29/1997	7.078	0.4582
07/02/1986	2.351	0.0077	06/03/1991	4.220	0.0065	05/30/1997	7.494	0.0552
07/10/1986	1.614	0.0008	06/03/1991	3.965	0.0121	05/30/1997	7.447	0.0853
07/16/1986	1.303	0.0011	06/04/1991	5.183	0.0265	05/30/1997	8.864	0.2432
05/13/1987	1.756	0.0074	06/04/1991	5.381	0.0212	05/31/1997	7.780	0.0880
05/22/1987	1.869	0.0109	06/11/1991	4.050	0.0043	05/31/1997	8.125	0.1412

USDA Forest Service RMRS-GTR-189. 2007

Date			Date			Date		
05/28/1987	3.002	0.0515	06/11/1991	4.050	0.0059	05/31/1997	9.421	0.2498
06/03/1987	2.096	0.0091	06/11/1991	4.078	0.0051	06/01/1997	10.302	0.2001
05/12/1988	1.926	0.0057	06/11/1991	4.475	0.0046	06/01/1997	10.050	0.1831
05/18/1988	4.418	0.0162	06/12/1991	4.248	0.0095	06/01/1997	9.862	0.1397
05/27/1988	4.220	0.0108	06/12/1991	3.936	0.0086	06/04/1997	11.243	0.9144
06/03/1988	2.124	0.0112	06/12/1991	4.191	0.0050	06/05/1997	9.950	0.8352
06/10/1988	1.671	0.0010	06/12/1991	4.361	0.0072	06/05/1997	10.025	1.0060
06/15/1988	1.359	0.0011	06/12/1991	4.503	0.0063	06/05/1997	11.158	1.0782
06/22/1988	1.161	0.0005	06/12/1991	4.701	0.0075	06/05/1997	11.561	1.4296
05/05/1989	2.379	0.0098	06/13/1991	4.418	0.0049	06/06/1997	9.723	0.5608
05/09/1989	4.899	0.0603	06/13/1991	4.305	0.0032	06/06/1997	9.295	0.6310
05/18/1989	4.361	0.0623	06/13/1991	4.135	0.0093	06/10/1997	7.233	0.4304
05/25/1989	3.880	0.0409	06/05/1992	0.736	0.0000	06/11/1997	6.137	0.4902
06/02/1989	3.370	0.0043	06/06/1992	0.736	0.0001	06/11/1997	6.137	0.5676
06/07/1989	4.701	0.0306	06/07/1992	0.708	0.0002	06/11/1997	6.039	0.5871
06/15/1989	3.455	0.0039	06/08/1992	0.708	0.0001	06/12/1997	5.642	0.1095
06/21/1989	2.209	0.0015	05/26/1993	5.551	0.0428	06/12/1997	5.504	0.0886
06/29/1989	1.473	0.0001	05/26/1993	5.154	0.0774	06/12/1997	5.689	0.1112
07/05/1989	1.274	0.0001	05/27/1993	6.145	0.0217	06/13/1997	5.089	0.0581
04/27/1990	1.529	0.0027	05/27/1993	6.259	0.0248	06/13/1997	4.918	0.0499

Appendix B—Piecewise regression results with bootstrap confidence intervals.

Watershed	Parameter	Estimate	Lower 95% CI	Upper 95% CI
East St. Louis Ck	SE	0.0098	0.0074	0.0115
	a_1	-0.0023	-0.0047	-0.0010
	b_1	0.0109	0.0072	0.0174
	b_2	0.0735	0.0442	0.1367
	c_1	0.7572	0.6733	0.8933
Fool Creek	SE	0.0050	0.0037	0.0061
	a_1	-0.0009	-0.0014	0.0002
	b_1	0.0172	0.0044	0.0227
	b_2	0.0856	0.0653	0.1061
	c_1	0.2211	0.1696	0.2580
Little Granite Ck	SE	0.1609	0.1253	0.1912
	a_1	-0.0037	-0.0330	-0.0003
	b_1	0.0043	0.0024	0.0173
	b_2	0.1046	0.0753	0.1851
	c_1	4.8446	4.1345	6.9900
Site 1	SE	0.0539	0.0383	0.0646
	a_1	-0.0055	-0.0157	0.0013
	b_1	0.0139	0.0074	0.0223
	b_2	0.0730	0.0454	0.1472
	c_1	3.4118	2.4869	4.6944
Site 2	SE	0.0549	0.0382	0.0686
	a_1	-0.0069	-0.0180	-0.0026
	b_1	0.0118	0.0086	0.0192
	b_2	0.1222	0.0941	0.2159
	c_1	4.4992	4.3024	5.4983
Site 3	SE	0.0702	0.0398	0.0940
	a_1	-0.0187	-0.0283	-0.0046
	b_1	0.0198	0.0080	0.0265
	b_2	0.0775	0.0432	0.1565
	c_1	4.0421	2.5055	4.9058

Watershed	Parameter	Estimate	Lower 95% CI	Upper 95% CI
Site 4	SE	0.0222	0.0170	0.0263
	a_1	-0.000004	-0.0069	0.0098
	b_1	0.0037	-0.0037	0.0092
	b_2	0.0228	0.0185	0.0318
	c_1	1.8972	1.6442	2.5725
Site 4a	SE	0.0299	0.0230	0.0353
	a_1	-0.0101	-0.0182	0.0085
	b_1	0.0124	-0.0001	0.0173
	b_2	0.0515	0.0368	0.0679
	c_1	2.8074	2.1699	3.1024
Site 5	SE	0.0142	0.0090	0.0179
	a_1	-0.00001	-0.0027	0.0031
	b_1	0.0036	0.0014	0.0057
	b_2	0.0437	0.0301	0.0811
	c_1	2.3545	2.1424	2.6587

(numbers highlighted are those where the intercept is not significantly different from zero and could be removed from model).